Name That
MOVIE!

A PAINLESS VOCABULARY BUILDER

Name That MOVIE!

A PAINLESS VOCABULARY BUILDER

Watch Movies and Ace
the *SAT, ACT®, GED®, and GRE®!

Brian Leaf, M.A.

Wiley Publishing, Inc.

*Name That Movie! A Painless Vocabulary Builder: Comedy & Action Edition: Watch Movies and Ace the *SAT, ACT®, GED®, and GRE®!*

Published by Wiley Publishing, Inc., Hoboken, New Jersey

For general information on our other products and services or to obtain technical support please contact our Customer Care Department within the U.S. at (877) 762-2974, outside the U.S. at (317) 572-3993 or fax (317) 572-4002.

Wiley also publishes its books in a variety of electronic formats. Some content that appears in print may not be available in electronic books. For more information about Wiley products, please visit our web site at www.wiley.com.

Library of Congress Cataloging-in-Publication Data:
Leaf, Brian.
 Name that movie! : a painless vocabulary builder : comedy & action edition : watch movies and ace the SAT, ACT, GED, and GRE! / Brian Leaf.
    p. cm.
    ISBN: 978-0-470-90325-4 (pbk.); ISBN: 978-0-470-92214-9 (ebk)
  1. Vocabulary--Study guides. 2. English language--Glossaries, vocabularies, etc. 3. Educational tests and measurements--Study guides. 4. Comedy films--Quotations, maxims, etc. 5. Action and adventure films--Quotations, maxims, etc. I. Title.
 PE1449.L325 2011
 428.1'076--dc22
   2010039045

Printed in the United States of America

10 9 8 7 6 5 4 3 2 1

Book production by Wiley Publishing, Inc., Composition Services

Acknowledgments

Thanks to my agents, Todd Shuster and Colleen Rafferty, and my fantastic editors at Wiley, Greg Tubach and Carol Pogoni. Thanks to Amy Sell and Adrienne Fontaine at Wiley for getting the word out. Thanks to Pam Weber-Leaf for great editing tips, Zach Nelson for sage marketing advice, Ian Curtis for assiduous proofreading, Manny and Susan Leaf for everything, and of course, thanks most of all to Gwen, Noah, and Benjamin for love, support, and inspiration.

About the Author

Brian Leaf, M.A., is the author of the four-book *Defining Twilight* vocabulary workbook series as well as the four-book SAT and ACT test-prep series *McGraw-Hill's Top 50 Skills for a Top Score*. He is Director of the New Leaf Learning Center in Massachusetts, and has provided SAT, ACT, GED, SSAT, and GRE preparation to thousands of students throughout the United States. For more information, visit his Web site at www.brianleaf.com.

How to Use This Book

This book contains 100 excerpts from comedy or action movies. For each excerpt, see if you can name the movie, describe the scene(s), and define the boldfaced vocabulary words. If you need help naming a movie, check the hint at the bottom of the page. Then check your answers against the definitions provided in this book. To help you memorize new words in each group, copy or say each vocabulary word and its synonyms five times and reread the movie excerpt. Also, after every ten groups, take the two-page quiz that tests definitions, synonyms, and even word parts that you've learned. There's no easier or more fun way to learn more than 1,000 words for the SAT, ACT, GED, or GRE. By the end of this book, your vocabulary will be larger, your test scores will be higher, and you'll be a *Superbad* vocabulary scholar!

Group 1

Here's an excerpt from a movie. See if you can name the movie, describe the scene, and define the boldface vocabulary words. Check your answers on the following page.

Jim: I should be able to talk to girls. I'm **articulate.** You know I got a 720 on my SAT verbal. (*Jim demonstrates his vocabulary.*) **Copious. Verisimilitude. Xenophobic.**

(*The audience hears the sound of a girl screaming upstairs. The screamer comes running through the kitchen with a vomit stain on her shirt. She bolts out the door and into the night. A moment passes.*)

Jim: **Regurgitation.**

Movie: _____

Scene: _____

_____

Articulate might mean _____

_____

Copious might mean _____

_____

Verisimilitude might mean _____

_____

Xenophobic might mean _____

_____

Regurgitation might mean _____

_____

Hint: "Like warm apple pie."

Solutions

Let's see how you did. Check your answers and write the exact definitions. To help you memorize the vocabulary words, reread the movie excerpt or even act out the scene with a friend.

Movie: *American Pie*, Universal Studios, 1999

Scene: Jim (Jason Biggs) and his friends are at a party at Stifler's house at the beginning of the movie.

Inside Scoop: The "pale ale" responsible for Stifler's **regurgitation** is actually beer with egg whites in it. This was Seann William Scott's (Stifler) first movie.

Articulate means *well spoken—able to express ideas clearly*. Jim is pretty articulate, unless he's speaking to Nadia (Shannon Elizabeth), the Czechoslovakian exchange student. Jim's dad (Eugene Levy) is also articulate, and I'd say probably the funniest dad character in any movie. Synonym: eloquent.

Copious means *plentiful*. Synonyms: abundant, bountiful, profuse, prolific. Antonym: sparse. Standardized tests frequently use *copious* and its synonyms. Remember to say or write every new vocabulary word and its synonyms five times. The repetition will help you learn and memorize the words. It's a great tip because you get to memorize a bunch of new words all at one time.

Verisimilitude means the appearance of being real and is an interesting word to break apart. *Veri-* comes from the Latin word *veritas* and means *truth,* and *similitude* means *similarity*. So, *verisimilitude* means **similarity to being true**—*the appearance of being real*. *Veri-* reminds me of Professor Snape's **truth** serum, **Verita**serum, which causes a person to only speak the **truth** in the *Harry Potter* books and movies. Synonyms: credibility, plausibility.

Xenophobic means *afraid of foreigners*. In fact, *xeno-* means *foreigners,* and *phobic* means *afraid of.*

Regurgitation means *vomiting*. The prefix *re-* means *again,* like tasting food **again**. OK, that was way too gross, but this *is* the *American Pie* page, so nothing is off-limits.

Group 2

Here's an excerpt from a movie. See if you can name the movie, describe the scene, and define the boldface vocabulary words. Check your answers on the following page.

NARRATOR: Then, the passing of a **titan.** Howard Stark's lifelong friend and ally, Obadiah Stane, steps in to help fill the gap left by the legendary founder, until at age 21, the **prodigal** son returns and is **anointed** the new CEO of Stark Industries. With the keys to the kingdom, Tony **ushers in** a new **era** for his father's **legacy** creating smarter weapons, advanced robotics . . .

RHODEY: As **liaison** to Stark Industries, I have had the unique privilege of serving with a real patriot. He is my friend, and he is my great **mentor.** Ladies and gentlemen, it is my honor to present this year's **Apogee** Award to Mr. Tony Stark.

Movie: _____

Scene: _____

Titan might mean _____

Prodigal might mean _____

Anointed might mean _____

Ushers in might mean _____

Era might mean _____

Legacy might mean _____

Liaison might mean _____

Mentor might mean _____

Apogee might mean _____

Hint: Stark Industries.

Solutions

Let's see how you did. Check your answers and write the exact definitions. To help you memorize the vocabulary words, reread the movie excerpt or even act out the scene with a friend.

Movie: *Iron Man,* Paramount Pictures, 2008

Scene: Early in the movie, Rhodey (Terrence Howard) is introducing Tony (Robert Downey, Jr.) at an awards ceremony.

Titan means *person of tremendous power or significance* and comes from Greek mythology, in which Titans are the parents of the gods.

Prodigal can mean *wasteful or overly extravagant. Prodigal son* is an *allusion* (reference) to a *parable* (moral story) in the Bible. The **prodigal** son left home and lived a **wastefully extravagant** lifestyle, but then returned home and repented. Synonym: profligate.

Anointed sounds like *appointed* and can mean ***appointed*** *to a powerful or important position*. Interestingly, *anointed* comes from the religious practice of smearing oil on priests or kings before they are **appointed** or sworn in.

Ushers in means *begins* or *guides in,* just like an **usher** might **guide** you to your seat at a concert or baseball game. Synonym: heralds.

Era means *time period of history.* Synonyms: eon, epoch.

Legacy means *something passed down.* Synonym: heritage.

Liaison means *representative* or *ambassador. Liaison* has a second meaning that standardized tests sometimes use; it can also mean *a secret love affair.*

Mentor means *teacher or guide.*

Apogee means *highest point.* The word *apogee* and its synonyms are often used in the name of awards that honor the **highest point** of achievement in a field or pursuit. Synonyms: acme, apex, climax, peak, pinnacle, zenith. Antonyms: nadir, perigee.

Group 3

Here's an excerpt from a movie. See if you can name the movie, describe the scene, and define the boldface vocabulary word. Check your answers on the following page.

PETER: Kids, your mother and I have decided that we are gonna help you two get out into the dating world.

LOIS: That's right. Chris, I'm gonna show you how to be an **affable,** desirable young man who doesn't smell like the inside of a wool hat.

Movie: _____

Scene: _____

_____

Affable might mean _____

_____

Hint: "You know what really grinds my gears?"

Solutions

Let's see how you did. Check your answers and write the exact definition. To help you memorize the vocabulary word, reread the movie excerpt or even act out the scene with a friend.

Movie: *Family Guy Presents Stewie Griffin: The Untold Story,* 20th Century Fox, 2005

Scene: After Chris and Meg interrupt their parents, who are trying to get intimate, Peter and Lois decide to teach the kids how to date, hoping to get them out of the house more often.

Inside Scoop: Did you realize that Seth Green (of *Austin Powers* and *The Italian Job*) and Mila Kunis (of *Forgetting Sarah Marshall* and *That '70s Show*) are the voices of Chris and Meg?

Affable means *friendly and easy to hang out with.* Lois teaches Chris about kissing, cuddling, and eating at a fancy restaurant. Peter, on the other hand, instructs Meg in the fine points of shaving a man's back and tolerating his gas. Peter is a righteous ladies' man, there's no doubt about that. Synonyms: amiable, amicable, cordial, genial, gregarious, simpatico.

Group 4

Here's an excerpt from a movie. See if you can name the movie, describe the scene, and define the boldface vocabulary word. Check your answers on the following page.

BEANIE: Gentlemen, we are discussing a brand new way to look at a fraternity. In other words, you need to forget about all the normal rules that apply to both college and society. Because this is a very big idea, my friends. We are talking about a non-exclusive, **egalitarian** brotherhood where community status and, more importantly, age have no bearing whatsoever.

Movie: _____

Scene: _____

_____

Egalitarian might mean _____

_____

Hint: This movie was directed by Todd Phillips, who also directed _The Hangover_.

Solutions

Let's see how you did. Check your answers and write the exact definition. To help you memorize the vocabulary word, reread the movie excerpt or even act out the scene with a friend.

Movie: *Old School*, DreamWorks, 2003

Scene: Mitch (Luke Wilson) and Frank (Will Ferrell) come home to Mitch's house to find Beanie (Vince Vaughn) describing his vision for a new fraternity to a roomful of hopeful pledges.

Inside Scoop: Todd Phillips, who directed *Old School* as well as *The Hangover*, makes a cameo in both movies. *Old School* also features *cameos* (small roles) by these *Hangover* characters: Dr. Walsh from the hospital; the woman from the front desk of Caesar's Palace Hotel; Eddie Palermo, who owns the "Best Little Wedding Chapel"; and the outrageous lead singer of the band that plays at Doug's wedding!

Egalitarian comes from the word *equal* and refers to *the belief that all people are equal and deserve equal rights*. Synonym: democratic.

Group 5

Here are two excerpts from a movie. See if you can name the movie, describe the scenes, and define the boldface vocabulary words. Check your answers on the following page.

MR. BREEN: Mr. Hughes, members of the committee, I have reviewed Mr. Hughes' photoplay entitled *The Outlaw* and I can state **categorically** that I have never seen anything quite so unacceptable as the shots of the mammaries of the character named Rio. For almost half the picture, the girl's mammaries, which are quite large and prominent, are shockingly uncovered. For this reason, I have concluded that the picture appeals only to **prurient** interests and should be denied the Motion Picture Association's seal of approval.

———————

HOWARD: I am supposed to be many things which are not complimentary. I am supposed to be **capricious.** I have been called a playboy. I've even been called an **eccentric,** but I do not believe I have the reputation of being a liar. Needless to say, the Hercules was a monumental undertaking. It is the largest plane ever built. It is over five stories tall with a wingspan longer than a football field.

Movie: _____

Scenes: _____

_____

Categorically might mean _____

Prurient might mean _____

Capricious might mean _____

Eccentric might mean _____

Hint: "A true **pioneer** of the world's airways."

Solutions

Let's see how you did. Check your answers and write the exact definitions. To help you memorize the vocabulary words, reread the movie excerpts or even act out the scenes with a friend.

Movie: *The Aviator,* Warner Bros., 2004

Scenes: In the first excerpt, Howard Hughes (Leonardo DiCaprio) appears in front of the Motion Picture Association to get their seal of approval for a film he is making. In the second excerpt, Hughes appears in front of a congressional hearing that is investigating his business activities.

Inside Scoop: Howard Hughes—adventurer, billionaire, inventor, and playboy—was the inspiration for Tony Stark's character in *Iron Man.*

Vocabulary in the Hint: The hint, "a true pioneer of the world's airways," is a line from the movie that describes Howard Hughes, and hints at the title of the film, *The Aviator. Pioneer* means *originator* or *first developer.* Standardized tests love the word *progenitor* as a synonym for *pioneer.*

Categorically means *absolutely* or *explicitly.* Synonyms: unequivocally, unqualifiedly. *Qualifiedly* can mean *with reservation,* so *unqualifiedly* means *without reservation—subject to no conditions—absolutely.*

Prurient means *excessively sexual,* such as mammaries "which are quite large and prominent" being "shockingly uncovered" for "almost half the picture." Believe it or not, I've actually seen the word *prurient* on the SAT. Standardized tests would never use the word *sex,* but *prurient* doesn't sound nearly as scandalous! Synonyms: concupiscent, lascivious, lewd, libidinous, licentious, lubricious, salacious.

Capricious means *unpredictable* or *changing too easily.* Synonyms: erratic, fickle, mercurial.

Eccentric in this case means *an unconventional or odd person.* It can also be used as an adjective to describe such a person. Synonyms: idiosyncratic, nonconformist.

Group 6

Here are two excerpts from a movie. See if you can name the movie, describe the scenes, and define the boldface vocabulary words. Check your answers on the following page.

W: . . . does your **depravity** know no bounds?

H: No . . . It's the most **apt** prediction Flora's made in years and precisely the reason you can't find a suitable ring.

W: Do you have my money?

H: You are terrified of a life without the thrill of the **macabre**. Admit it.

(*Note:* Because these characters' names would give away the title of the movie, I have used only the initials of their last names.)

_____

Sir Thomas: Be as skeptical as you like, but our secret systems have steered the world towards a greater good for centuries. Their danger is they can also be used for more **nefarious** purposes.

Movie: _____

Scenes: _____

_____

Depravity might mean _____

Apt might mean _____

Macabre might mean _____

Nefarious might mean _____

Hint: "I was trying to **deduce** the manner in which Blackwood survived his execution. Clearing your good name, as it were. But it had a surprisingly **soporific** effect on me, and I was carried off in the arms of **Morpheus**, like a caterpillar in a cocoon."

Solutions

Let's see how you did. Check your answers and write the exact definitions. To help you memorize the vocabulary words, reread the movie excerpts or even act out the scenes with a friend.

Movie: *Sherlock Holmes*, Warner Bros., 2009

Scenes: In the first excerpt, Holmes (Robert Downey, Jr.) and Watson (Jude Law) are following a clue that leads them to a pawnshop. As they approach the pawnshop, a fortune teller predicts bad things for Watson's impending marriage, but Watson realizes that Holmes put the fortune teller up to it. In the second excerpt, Holmes has been taken to the headquarters of a secret society known as the Temple of the Four Orders. The society asks Holmes to find and stop Lord Blackwood (Mark Strong), whom they believe plans to use their secret systems for *nefarious* (evil) purposes.

Vocabulary in the Hint: *Deduce* means *conclude by logic.* Sherlock Holmes is famous for using this word, which makes sense since he is a huge fan of logic. *Soporific* is a high-level word that means *sleep inducing.* Synonyms: somniferous, somnolent. *Morpheus* refers to the *Greek god of dreams.* Morpheus is the son of *Somnus,* the *Roman god of sleep,* and interestingly, the synonyms for *soporific* (sleep inducing) resemble **Somn**us: **somn**olent and **somn**iferous!

Depravity means *immorality.* Synonyms: corruption, debauchery, degeneracy, deviance, dissipation, indecency, iniquity, lechery, licentiousness, obscenity, perversion, profligacy, prurience, turpitude, vice. Do you remember *prurient* from *The Aviator* scene in Group 5? The Motion Picture Association called Howard Hughes' movie, *The Outlaw,* too *prurient* (immoral, excessively sexual) due to its excessive close-up shots of Jane Russell's "mammaries."

Apt means *appropriate, likely,* or *able.* Synonyms: apposite, apropos, germane, pertinent.

Macabre means *deathly and horrifying.* Synonyms: ghastly, gory, grisly, grotesque, gruesome, hideous, morbid.

Nefarious means *wicked.* Synonyms: baleful, depraved, heinous, impious, iniquitous, malevolent, pernicious.

Group 7

Here's an excerpt from a movie. See if you can name the movie, describe the scene, and define the boldface vocabulary words. Check your answers on the following page.

||||||||||||||||||||||||||||||||||||||||||||||||||

FASHION INDUSTRY *SYNDICATE:* We need an empty **vessel** . . . a shallow, dumb, **vacuous** moron . . .

MUGATU: But who? I mean where in all of God's green goodness am I going to find someone that beef-headed?

||||||||||||||||||||||||||||||||||||||||||||||||||

Movie: _____

Scene: _____

_____

Syndicate might mean _____

_____

Vessel might mean _____

_____

Vacuous might mean _____

_____

Hint: "I'm not an **ambi**-turner . . . I can't turn left."

Solutions

Let's see how you did. Check your answers and write the exact definitions. To help you memorize the vocabulary words, reread the movie excerpt or even act out the scene with a friend.

Movie: *Zoolander*, Paramount Pictures, 2001

Scene: *Zoolander* opens with a news broadcast stating, "Here in Malaysia, there is an almost overwhelming sense of **euphoria** as the newly elected prime minister has given this nation a gift of hope, promising to raise the substandard minimum wage and end child labor once and for all." The newly elected prime minister's plans bring *euphoria* (extreme excitement) to the country, but terrify the evil Fashion Industry Syndicate, which stands to lose money from the new child-labor law. Therefore, the syndicate pressures fashion *mogul* (powerful person) Jacobim Mugatu (Will Ferrell) to train an operative to assassinate the Malaysian prime minister.

Vocabulary in the Hint: Derek Zoolander (Ben Stiller) tells Matilda (Christine Taylor) that he is not an ambi-turner, meaning he can't turn *both* ways while modeling. *Ambi-* means *both* as in *ambiguous* (unclear, open to **more than one** interpretation) and *ambivalent* (having mixed feelings, undecided between the **two** sides of an issue). Derek has never been able to turn left; that's his private, shameful secret.

Syndicate means *an association of people promoting similar interests. Syn-* means *united* as in *synthesis* (the **uniting** of parts into a whole).

Vessel means *container,* as in blood vessel.

Vacuous means *mindless* or *empty,* like a *vacuum* (totally empty space) in science class. Synonyms: fatuous, inane, insipid, vacant, vapid. Antonym: intelligent. After Mugatu declares his need for a "dumb, vacuous moron," you are introduced to veteran model Derek Zoolander, three-time Male Model of the Year. Zoolander is defending his title from young upstart Hansel (Owen Wilson).

Group 8

Here's an excerpt from a movie. See if you can name the movie, describe the scene, and define the boldface vocabulary words. Check your answers on the following page.

Bruce: People need dramatic examples to shake them out of **apathy,** and . . . as a symbol I can be **incorruptible,** I can be **everlasting.**

Alfred: What symbol?

Bruce: Something **elemental,** something terrifying.

Alfred: I assume that as you're taking on the underworld, this symbol is a persona to protect those you care about from **reprisals.**

Bruce: You are thinking about Rachel?

Alfred: Actually, sir, I was thinking of myself.

Bruce: Have you told anyone I'm coming back?

Alfred: I just couldn't figure the legal **ramifications** of bringing you back from the dead.

Movie: _____

Scene: _____

Apathy might mean _____

Incorruptible might mean _____

Everlasting might mean _____

Elemental might mean _____

Reprisals might mean _____

Ramifications might mean _____

Hint: Michael Keaton, Val Kilmer, George Clooney, and Christian Bale have each played this role.

Solutions

Let's see how you did. Check your answers and write the exact definitions. To help you memorize the vocabulary words, reread the movie excerpt or even act out the scene with a friend.

Movie: *Batman Begins,* Warner Bros., 2005

Scene: Bruce Wayne (Christian Bale) and Alfred (Michael Caine) are traveling back to Gotham while Bruce plots how best to fight injustice.

Apathy means *lack of interest.* This is an interesting word to break apart. *A-* means *without* and *path-* refers to *feeling,* so *apathy* means *without feeling—lack of interest.* Synonyms: dispassion, ennui, indifference, insouciance.

Incorruptible means *indestructible.* Synonyms: enduring, everlasting, imperishable, indissoluble.

Everlasting means *lasting forever.* It is a synonym for *incorruptible* because something that is **indestructible** will **last forever.** The opposite of *everlasting* is *temporary* along with its awesome synonyms *ephemeral, evanescent, fleeting, fugitive, impermanent, transient,* and *transitory. Fugitive* reminds me of the 1993 movie, *The Fugitive,* in which Harrison Ford is running from the law, moving quickly from place to place, staying in one place only **temporarily.**

Elemental means *representing the power of nature.* It can also mean *essential* or *basic,* as in the **elemental** components of water.

Reprisals means *acts of revenge or payback.* Synonyms: requital, retaliation, retribution, vengeance.

Ramifications means *consequences, usually negative.*

Group 9

Here's an excerpt from a movie. See if you can name the movie, describe the scene, and define the boldface vocabulary words. Check your answers on the following page.

D.E.: The details of my life are quite **inconsequential** . . . Very well, where do I begin? My father was a **relentlessly** self-improving **boulangerie** owner from Belgium with low-grade **narcolepsy** and a **penchant** for . . . Sometimes he would accuse chestnuts of being lazy, the sort of general **malaise** that only the genius possess and the insane **lament.** My childhood was typical. Summers in Rangoon, luge lessons. In the spring we'd make meat helmets. When I was **insolent** I was placed in a burlap bag and beaten with reeds—pretty standard really. At the age of twelve I received my first **scribe.**

Movie: _____

Scene: _____

Inconsequential might mean _____

Relentlessly might mean _____

Boulangerie might mean _____

Narcolepsy might mean _____

Penchant might mean _____

Malaise might mean _____

Lament might mean _____

Insolent might mean _____

Scribe might mean _____

Hint: "Shagadelic!"

Solutions

Let's see how you did. Check your answers and write the exact definitions. To help you memorize the vocabulary words, reread the movie excerpt or even act out the scene with a friend.

Movie: *Austin Powers: International Man of Mystery,* New Line Cinema, 1997

Scene: Dr. Evil (Mike Myers) and his son, Scott Evil (Seth Green), are in group therapy together. The therapist says, "Tell us a little about yourself," prompting this hilarious response from Dr. Evil.

Inconsequential means *not important.* This is a cool word to break apart. *In-* means *not,* like *inconsistent* or *ineffective,* and *consequential* means *having consequences*—that's why *inconsequential* means *not having consequences,* or *unimportant.*

Relentlessly means *constantly* or *tirelessly.* Synonyms: incessantly, inexorably, interminably, unremitting.

Boulangerie means *bakery* in French.

Narcolepsy refers to *the disorder of falling asleep uncontrollably whenever relaxed.*

Penchant means *fondness for* or *tendency.* Synonyms: knack, predilection, proclivity.

Malaise means *unhappiness.* Synonym: melancholy.

Lament means *grieve,* as in "The **Lament** for Gandalf" sung by the elves in *The Lord of the Rings: The Fellowship of the Ring* after Gandalf falls into an *abyss* (deep pit) during his fight with the Balrog.

Insolent sounds like *insult* and means *rudely disrespectful.* Professor Snape often calls Harry Potter *insolent.* Synonyms: cheeky, contemptuous, contumelious, impertinent, impudent, insubordinate, pert, sassy, saucy.

Scribe means *a secretary* or *any person who writes.* Most words that contain *scrib-* are about *writing* such as *circumscribe* (**write** around something, confine and restrict) and *transcribe* (copy or put thoughts, notes, or speech into **writing**).

Group 10

Here's an excerpt from a movie. See if you can name the movie, describe the scene, and define the boldface vocabulary words. Check your answers on the following page.

Jor-El: These **indictments** that I have brought to you today, the specific charges listed herein against the individuals—their acts of **treason,** their ultimate aim of **sedition**—*these* are matters of undeniable fact. I ask you now to pronounce judgment on those accused. On this, this mindless **aberration,** whose only means of expression are **wanton** violence and destruction; on the woman Ursa, whose **perversions** and unreasoning hatred of all mankind have threatened even the children of the planet Krypton; finally, General Zod, . . . chief architect of this intended revolution and author of this **insidious** plot to establish a new order amongst us, with himself as **absolute** ruler.

Movie: _____

Scene: _____

Indictments might mean _____

Treason might mean _____

Sedition might mean _____

Aberration might mean _____

Wanton might mean _____

Perversions might mean _____

Insidious might mean _____

Absolute might mean _____

Hint: Planet Krypton.

Solutions

Let's see how you did. Check your answers and write the exact definitions. To help you memorize the vocabulary words, reread the movie excerpt or even act out the scene with a friend.

Movie: *Superman,* Warner Bros., 1978

Scene: This scene is at the beginning of *Superman* when Jor-El (Marlon Brando) is accusing the three characters mentioned. You might not have seen this movie recently, but the "planet Krypton" reference is pretty much the giveaway.

Inside Scoop: The *Superman* films of the late 1970s and early 1980s are credited for bringing the superhero *genre* (category or type) of movies into mainstream theaters. So, apparently, if you enjoy the *Batman* and *X-Men* films, you've got *Superman* to thank!

Indictments means *accusations of wrongdoing.*

Treason means *disloyalty to one's country.* Synonyms: perfidy, sedition.

Sedition means *inciting rebellion.* Synonyms: insurgence, insurrection, mutiny, perfidy, subversion, treason.

Aberration means *abnormality* and can, as in this case, mean specifically *a person who behaves in an unacceptable and **abnormal** way.* Synonyms: anomaly, deviation, divergence, perversion.

Wanton means *deliberate and spiteful.* It can also mean *promiscuous.*

Perversions means *misuse or corruption of things,* like what was done to Mike Tyson's tiger, what Stu did to his tooth, or pretty much anything that was done during the night in *The Hangover.*

Insidious in this case means *treacherous and clever.* Synonyms: crafty, cunning, shifty, sly, wily.

Absolute means *total* or *complete.* Synonyms: categorical, consummate, unconditional, unmitigated, unqualified.

Quiz 1

I. Let's review some of the words that you've seen in Groups 1–10. Match each of the following words to the correct definition or synonym on the right. If you need help, refer back to the movie excerpts and definitions. Then check the solutions on page 233.

1. Copious
2. Verisimilitude
3. Prodigal
4. Apogee
5. Affable
6. Egalitarian
7. Prurient
8. Capricious
9. Depravity
10. Macabre
11. Nefarious
12. Soporific
13. Vacuous
14. Ramifications
15. Penchant

A. Wasteful
B. Amiable
C. Excessively sexual
D. Mercurial
E. Acme
F. Credibility
G. Vice
H. Sleep-inducing
I. Plentiful
J. Equal
K. Consequences
L. Pernicious
M. Morbid
N. Predilection
O. Fatuous

II. Let's review several of the word parts that you've seen in Groups 1–10. Match each of the following word parts to the correct definition or synonym on the right. Then check the solutions on page 233.

16. Veri- (as in *verisimilitude*)
17. Xeno- (as in *xenophobic*)
18. Ambi- (as in *ambiguous*)
19. Syn- (as in *syndicate*)
20. Path- (as in *apathy*)
21. Scribe- (as in *circumscribe*)

A. United
B. Both
C. Write
D. Foreigners
E Truth
F. Feeling

21

Quiz 1 (continued)

III. Match each group of synonyms to its general meaning. Then check the solutions on page 233.

22. Abundant
    Bountiful
    Copious
    Profuse
    Prolific

    A. Wicked

23. Affable
    Amiable
    Amicable
    Cordial
    Genial
    Gregarious
    Simpatico

    B. Constant, tireless

24. Baleful
    Depraved
    Heinous
    Impious
    Iniquitous
    Malevolent
    Nefarious
    Pernicious

    C. Lack of interest

25. Fatuous
    Inane
    Insipid
    Vacuous
    Vapid

    D. Friendly

26. Apathy
    Dispassion
    Indifference
    Insouciance

    E. Plentiful

27. Incessant
    Inexorable
    Interminable
    Relentless
    Unremitting

    F. Mindless

Group 11

Here's an excerpt from a movie. See if you can name the movie, describe the scene, and define the boldface vocabulary words. Check your answers on the following page.

JAMES: So you're a cadet. You're studying. What's your focus?

UHURA: **Xenolinguistics.** (*short pause*) You have no idea what that means.

JAMES: The study of alien languages, **morphology, phonology, syntax.** Means you've got a talented tongue.

Movie: _____

Scene: _____

_____

Xenolinguistics might mean _____

_____

Morphology might mean _____

_____

Phonology might mean _____

_____

Syntax might mean _____

_____

Hint: Uhura winds up becoming Chief Communications Officer aboard the USS *Enterprise*.

Solutions

Let's see how you did. Check your answers and write the exact definitions. To help you memorize the vocabulary words, reread the movie excerpt or even act out the scene with a friend.

Movie: *Star Trek,* Paramount Pictures, 2009

Scene: Young, rebellious Kirk (Chris Pine) meets Uhura (Zoe Saldana) in a bar and is hitting on her. Always quite the ladies man, Kirk impresses her with his vocabulary (and now you can impress with your new vocabulary, too, thanks to *Name That Movie!*).

Xenolinguistics means *the study of alien languages. Xeno-* means *alien or foreign,* as in *xenophobic* (afraid of foreigners); *lingua* refers to *language;* and *-ics* means *study of.* That's why *xenolinguistics* means *the study of alien languages.*

Morphology, in the field of *linguistics* (the study of languages), means *the study of word forms and word relationships. Morph* means *form,* and *-logy,* like *-ics,* means *study of.* People use the word *morph* to mean *change,* but it actually means *form. Morph* is oftentimes used to mean *change* as an abbreviation for *meta**morph**osis,* which means **change** *of shape or form.*

Phonology means *the study of speech sounds of a language.* That makes sense since *phono-* means *sound* as in *phonograph* (old-style record player).

Syntax means *arranging words together to make well-formed sentences. Syn-* means *together,* as in *synergy* (cooperation) and the fashion industry *syndicate* (association) in *Zoolander.*

Group 12

Here's an excerpt from a movie. See if you can name the movie, describe the scene, and define the boldface vocabulary words. Check your answers on the following page.

MATILDA: I'm trying to talk to Mugatu but he's tougher to get to than the president.

DEREK: Oh . . . I thought you were going to tell me what a bad **eugooglizer** I am.

MATILDA: A what?

DEREK: A *eugooglizer . . . one who speaks at funerals.* Or did you think I would be too stupid to know what a **eugoogly** was?

Movie: _____

Scene: _____

_____

Eulogize might mean _____

_____

Eulogy might mean _____

_____

Hint: The Center For Kids Who Can't Read Good And Wanna Learn To Do Other Stuff Good, Too.

Solutions

Let's see how you did. Check your answers and write the exact definitions. To help you memorize the vocabulary words, reread the movie excerpt or even act out the scene with a friend.

Movie: *Zoolander,* Paramount Pictures, 2001

Scene: Matilda (Christine Taylor, Ben Stiller's real-life wife and the actress who played Marcia Brady in the *Brady Bunch* movies) is a journalist who approaches Zoolander (Ben Stiller) after he gives the eugoogly (Derek Zoolander's mispronunciation of *eulogy*) at his friends' funeral.

Eulogize means *praise, often in a speech at a funeral*. I've seen this word stump students on the SAT, but now you know it thanks to Derek Zoo-lander! Synonym: *extol*. The opposite of *eulogize* is *censure* (criticize severely).

Eulogy means *written or spoken praise, often at a funeral*. Derek is giving a eulogy for his friends who "died in a freak gasoline-fight accident" that occurred when they all went out for orange mocha frappuccinos to cheer up Derek after his loss of Male Model of the Year to Hansel (Owen Wilson). They got a bit frisky with the gasoline pumps, which led to a totally innocent gasoline fight, until, unfortunately, one of them lit a cigarette during the roughhousing.

Group 13

Here's an excerpt from a movie. See if you can name the movie, describe the scene, and define the boldface vocabulary word. Check your answers on the following page.

JAMES: Excuse me, soldier. You in charge of this area here?

SOLDIER: What's up?

JAMES: You know this guy? How do we know that he's not giving intel to **insurgents,** telling them where to drop mortars?

SOLDIER: I think he's just selling DVDs.

JAMES: Well, he's a security risk. We should get rid of him.

SOLDIER: He's just selling DVDs, man. All the merchants are clear.

Movie: _____

Scene: _____

_____

Insurgents might mean _____

_____

Hint: "The rush of battle is often a **potent** and **lethal** addiction, for war is a drug."

Solutions

Let's see how you did. Check your answers and write the exact definition. To help you memorize the vocabulary word, reread the movie excerpt or even act out the scene with a friend.

Movie: *The Hurt Locker,* Summit Entertainment, 2009

Scene: Staff Sergeant James (Jeremy Renner) befriends a young boy named "Beckham" (Christopher Sayegh), who sells pirated DVDs from a merchant's booth on the military base. James finds a dead boy and believes it is Beckham, so he is angry and looking for answers. In this scene, he approaches the merchant of the booth, but the merchant does not speak English, so he approaches the soldier who oversees the area.

Vocabulary in the Hint: *Potent* means *powerful.* Synonyms: formidable, puissant. *Lethal* means *deadly.*

Insurgents means *rebels.* Synonyms: agitators, insurrectionists, renegades, subversives. *Insurgents* and its synonyms come up frequently on standardized tests.

Group 14

Here are two excerpts from a movie. See if you can name the movie, describe the scenes, and define the boldface vocabulary words. Check your answers on the following page.

JOHN: What is the **extraction** plan for the prisoners?

GENERAL: Extraction plan? There is no extraction plan, we're going to level the place.

JOHN: Negative. I told you, SkyNet Central is filled with human prisoners.

KATE: It has a **hybrid** nervous system. One human **cortex,** one machine.

MARCUS: Blair, what have they done?

JOHN: Who built you?

MARCUS: My name is Marcus Wright.

JOHN: You think you're human?

MARCUS: I *am* human.

Movie: _____

Scenes: _____

_____

Extraction might mean _____

Hybrid might mean _____

Cortex might mean _____

Hint: "Early in the twenty-first century, SkyNet, a military defense program, became self-aware. Viewing humanity as a threat to its existence, SkyNet decided to strike first. The survivors of the nuclear fire called the event "Judgment Day." They lived only to face a new nightmare . . . the war against the machines. To hunt down and **eradicate** humans, SkyNet built . . ."

Solutions

Let's see how you did. Check your answers and write the exact definitions. To help you memorize the vocabulary words, reread the movie excerpts or even act out the scenes with a friend.

Movie: *Terminator Salvation,* Warner Bros., 2009

Scenes: In the first excerpt, John Connor (Christian Bale) is reporting to headquarters that the experimental signal to "turn off" the machines is operational, so the General orders an attack on SkyNet. In the second excerpt, Kate (Bryce Dallas Howard) explains to John what she has discovered about Marcus (Sam Worthington), who is actually half machine (Terminator) and half human.

Vocabulary in the Hint: *Eradicate* means *destroy completely.* Synonyms: annihilate, expunge, obliterate.

Extraction means *removal.*

Hybrid means *mixture,* in this case part human, part machine. Synonyms: amalgamation, composite, fusion.

Cortex translates as *bark* in Latin and refers, in this case, to *the outer layer of the front part of the brain,* so it's like the **bark** of the front part of the brain.

Group 15

Here's an excerpt from a movie. See if you can name the movie, describe the scene, and define the boldface vocabulary word. Check your answers on the following page.

PETE: Marriage is like that show *Everybody Loves Raymond,* but it's not funny. All the problems are the same, but, it's . . . you know, instead of all the funny, **pithy** dialogue, everybody is just really pissed off and tense.

Movie: _____

Scene: _____

_____

Pithy might mean _____

_____

Hint: Seth Rogen's first starring role in a movie. In Russia, this film's title translates to *A Little Bit Pregnant.*

Solutions

Let's see how you did. Check your answers and write the exact definition. To help you memorize the vocabulary word, reread the movie excerpt or even act out the scene with a friend.

Movie: *Knocked Up,* Universal Pictures, 2007

Scene: Ben (Seth Rogen) and Alison (Katherine Heigl) had a huge fight, so in this scene, Ben is hanging out with his friend, Pete (Paul Rudd), who is dispensing his *dispirited* (depressed) wisdom.

Inside Scoop: Ben's buddies are all named for the real first names of the actors who play them: Jason (Jason Segel), Jonah (Jonah Hill), Jay (Jay Baruchel), and Martin (Martin Starr). Also Ken Jeong, a physician who started doing stand-up comedy during his medical internship in New Orleans, plays Dr. Kuni, the gynecologist, but you know him better as Mr. Leslie Chow from *The Hangover!*

Pithy means *short and meaningful,* so "funny, pithy dialogue" is definitely a compliment to *Everybody Loves Raymond.* In fact, Judd Apatow (he directed, wrote, or produced this and so many other hilarious movies) must love *Everybody Loves Raymond*—he included episodes of the show in David's big box o' porn in *The 40-Year-Old Virgin,* he gave Ray Romano (who plays Raymond) a cameo in *Funny People,* and he referenced the show in *Knocked Up.* Synonyms for *pithy:* compendious, concise, crisp, epigrammatic, succinct, terse. Antonym: verbose.

Group 16

Here's an excerpt from a movie. See if you can name the movie, describe the scene, and define the boldface vocabulary words. Check your answers on the following page.

SYDNEY: I've found that at the classy open houses, the spread is usually pretty decent and there's a beautiful **bevy** of attractive and newly single women.

PETE: I don't know what to say. Thank you for your honesty.

SYDNEY: Thank you for the sundried tomato aioli, because it's a **revelation.**

PETE: Oh, wow! Hey, thanks for noticing.

SYDNEY: Yeah. All right, I'm going to take this panini for the road. There's an open house in Belle Air that promises to be **replete** with **cougars.**

Movie: _____

Scene: _____

_____

Bevy might mean _____

Revelation might mean _____

Replete might mean _____

Cougars might mean _____

Hint: "Peter, I am a man. I have an ocean of testosterone flowing through my veins. Society tells us we're civilized, but the truth is we are animals . . . Every once in a while I go down to the boardwalk, and I just throw my own feces like a gorilla."

Solutions

Let's see how you did. Check your answers and write the exact definitions. To help you memorize the vocabulary words, reread the movie excerpt or even act out the scene with a friend.

Movie: *I Love You, Man,* DreamWorks Pictures, 2009

Scene: Pete (Paul Rudd) doesn't have any male friends and is looking for a new friend to be his Best Man when he marries Zooey (Rashida Jones). He and Sydney (Jason Segel) have just met at an open house at Lou Ferrigno's mansion. Sydney gives Pete his card, and the bromance begins.

Bevy means *large group.* Synonyms: horde, throng.

Revelation means *surprising or dramatic announcement or realization,* like the truth has been **reveal**ed. Synonym: epiphany.

Replete means *full.*

Cougars is slang for *older women who seek out younger men.*

Group 17

Here's an excerpt from a movie. See if you can name the movie, describe the scene, and define the boldface vocabulary word. Check your answers on the following page.

DAVID: You're wound up. You're like one of these action figures all **hermetically** sealed in your box. (*Reaches to pick up a sealed action figure off a shelf.*) You've got to play with . . .

ANDY: Don't! Don't! Don't take it out! (*short pause*) I'm sorry. You know what? It's just, it loses its value if you take it out of its packaging.

DAVID: I'm just saying let it out. Give it some air, man. Play with it.

Movie: _____

Scene: _____

_____

Hermetically might mean _____

_____

Hint: "Andy, for the last time, I don't want your giant box of pornography!"

Solutions

Let's see how you did. Check your answers and write the exact definition. To help you memorize the vocabulary word, reread the movie excerpt or even act out the scene with a friend.

Movie: *The 40-Year-Old Virgin,* Universal Pictures, 2005

Scene: David (Paul Rudd) brought his big box o' porn as a gift for Andy (Steve Carell). Andy tries to reject the gift, but David insists on leaving it. Did you catch the *double entendre* (double meaning) in the dialogue?

Inside Scoop: This movie has some fun cameos. Did you notice actor Jonah Hill buying the sparkly, silver platform boots with fish in the heels in Trish's (Catherine Keener) eBay store? Now he's in everything (*Superbad, Forgetting Sarah Marshall, Knocked Up, Funny People*), but no one knew him when he appeared in *Virgin*. In fact, I believe this was his first appearance with the Judd Apatow gang. While we're at it, did you notice that Trish's daughter Marla, played by Kat Dennings, was Norah from *Nick and Norah's Infinite Playlist?* And lastly, we have Jane Lynch, who plays Paula, the store manager who wants to "mentor" the virgin (Andy) through his "transition." This was also her big breakout movie and led to roles in *Talladega Nights* (she plays Ricky Bobby's mother) and *Role Models* (she is the nutty manager of the big brother program). You probably also recognize her from the TV show *Glee* where she plays the slightly psycho cheerleading coach.

Hermetically means *completely sealed,* just like a person who is a **hermit** is *completely sealed off from the rest of the world.* The word *hermit* (loner) has lots of great high-level synonyms, such as *eremite, recluse,* and *troglodyte.* Another synonym is *anchoress* (which has nothing to do with female news **anchor** Veronica Corningstone, who, thanks to Ron Burgundy, is certainly no **hermit**).

Group 18

Here's an excerpt from a movie. See if you can name the movie, describe the scene, and define the boldface vocabulary words. Check your answers on the following page.

REMY: (*playing poker*) So, what brings you to our fair city, sir?

LOGAN: **Victor Creed.**

REMY: And who's that?

LOGAN: The man I'm gonna kill. He works with a man named Stryker on an island. Just need to know where it is.

REMY: And why would you think I know that?

LOGAN: Well, 'cause I know who you are, **Gambit.** You're the guy who escaped, and you're the guy who's gonna take me back there.

Movie: _____

Scene: _____

_____

Victor might mean _____

_____

Creed might mean _____

_____

Gambit might mean _____

_____

Hint: Logan's girlfriend, Kayla, has the skill of **tactile hypnosis.**

Solutions

Let's see how you did. Check your answers and write the exact definitions. To help you memorize the vocabulary words, reread the movie excerpt or even act out the scene with a friend.

Movie: *X-Men Origins: Wolverine,* 20th Century Fox, 2009

Scene: Logan (a.k.a. Wolverine, played by Hugh Jackman) finds Gambit (Taylor Kitsch) playing poker in a tavern.

Inside Scoop: The other player who is visible at the poker table is actually Daniel Negreanu, a real-life Canadian professional poker player and winner of four World Series of Poker bracelets and two World Poker Tour titles! He is also the star of TV's poker game show *Million Dollar Challenge.*

Vocabulary in the Hint: Logan's girlfriend Kayla (Lynn Collins) has the skill of **tactile hypnosis.** As Stryker (Danny Huston) says, "she can **influence** people as long as she **touches** them." *Hypnosis* refers to *an altered, sleep-like state that is very responsive to influence and suggestion,* and *tactile* means *touchable.* That's why Kayla's *tactile hypnosis* refers to the *ability to **influence** people that she **touches.*** Synonyms for *tactile:* corporeal, palpable, tangible. Standardized tests also love to test the fancy names for the other senses: taste = *gustation,* hearing = *audition,* smell = *olfaction.*

Victor is the first name of Logan's brother, but the word also means *winner* or *conqueror.* Synonym: vanquisher.

Creed means *set of beliefs.* Synonyms: canon, doctrine, dogma, ideology, precepts, tenets. So Victor's full name, *Victor Creed,* translates to *conqueror's set of beliefs.* That makes sense; Victor is brutal and cruel, and he's happiest when fighting and **conquering**—it's what he lives for and what defines him. As Wraith (played by rapper will.i.am) says, "He had to prove he was better than you, hunting and killing everything . . . "

Gambit means *a calculated risk taken to gain an advantage in a game, competition, or battle,* like sacrificing a piece in chess or bluffing in poker. *Gambit* is an appropriate mutant name for Remy, an ex-thief and avid gambler, who is playing poker when Wolverine meets him in the film. Synonyms: machination, maneuver, ploy, ruse, scheme, stratagem, tactic, wangle.

Group 19

Here's an excerpt from a movie. See if you can name the movie, describe the scene, and define the boldface vocabulary words. Check your answers on the following page.

(Aldous and Peter wander into one another while paddling on surfboards.)

ALDOUS SNOW: Hey, ahoy there.

PETER: You surf, too?

ALDOUS SNOW: No, goodness, I'm just drifting around, ya know, getting in touch with the ocean and stuff. It's really pleasant.

PETER: It was, yeah. Ah, I'm gonna head in.

ALDOUS SNOW: Before you go, actually, Peter, I wanted to tell you, I was listening to Sarah's iPod the other day, and amidst the **interminable dross** that's on that thing, I found one track that I quite liked. So I checked what it was, and it was actually one of yours, and it kind of reminded me of a dark, **gothic** Neil Diamond.

PETER: That's like *exactly* what I'm going for.

Movie: _____

Scene: _____

_____

Interminable might mean _____

_____

Dross might mean _____

_____

Gothic might mean _____

_____

Hint: This movie costars Mila Kunis.

Solutions

Let's see how you did. Check your answers and write the exact definitions. To help you memorize the vocabulary words, reread the movie excerpt or even act out the scene with a friend.

Movie: *Forgetting Sarah Marshall,* Universal Pictures, 2008

Scene: Peter (Jason Segel) meets Aldous (Russell Brand) while surfing. Aldous is dating Peter's ex-girlfriend Sarah Marshall, which is why Peter is not thrilled to have bumped into him.

Inside Scoop: You learned in a previous group that Mila Kunis (who plays Rachel in this film) is the voice of *Family Guy*'s Meg as well as Jackie on *That '70s Show.* Well, here's another gem. Kristen Bell, who plays Sarah Marshall, is the voice of the mysterious *Gossip Girl!*

Interminable means *endless. In-* means *not* and *terminable* means *ending,* so *interminable* means *unending—endless.* Synonyms: ceaseless, eternal, incessant. Antonym: ephemeral.

Dross comes from the word *dregs* and means *trash,* or *rubbish* as Aldous might say. Aldous means that most of the music on Sarah's iPod is *rubbish.* Synonyms: chaff, debris, detritus, dreck, flotsam.

Gothic means *dark or gloomy.* It also means *relating to the Goths of Eastern Europe during the **Dark** Ages.* So, Peter's music is like a **dark or gloomy** Neil Diamond. Aldous probably heard a ballad from Peter's Dracula opera/puppet show. It's hilarious when Rachel, not knowing what she's in for, makes him get up in front of everyone at the bar and belt one out. I love Peter's **dark and gloomy** Dracula voice complete with Transylvanian accent! Synonym: macabre.

Group 20

Here's an excerpt from a movie. See if you can name the movie, describe the scene, and define the boldface vocabulary word. Check your answers on the following page.

H: How long are we doing this?

MEDICINE WOMAN: Until you have an **epiphany.**

H: OK . . . What's an epiphany?

MEDICINE WOMAN: *Sudden realization of great truth.*

H: OK.

MEDICINE WOMAN: Unless you have an epiphany, you will spend the remainder of your days alone.

H: OK, epiphany, epiphany, epiphany . . . Oh! Bananas are an excellent source of potassium!

(*H gets slapped by the epiphatree.*)

Movie: _____

Scene: _____

_____

Epiphany might mean _____

_____

Hint: "D'oh!"

Solutions

Let's see how you did. Check your answers and write the exact definition. To help you memorize the vocabulary word, reread the movie excerpt or even act out the scene with a friend.

Movie: *The Simpsons Movie,* 20th Century Fox, 2007

Scene: Homer has been saved by an Inuit shaman medicine woman who helps him see what he must do. His epiphany is that "other people are just as important as me. Without them I'm nothing. In order to save myself, I have to save Springfield," so he sets off to save Springfield.

Inside Scoop: "What's an Epiphany?" is song #6 on *The Simpsons Movie* soundtrack along with classics "Spider Pig" and "Bart's Doodle."

Epiphany means *sudden realization of great truth.* Synonym: revelation.

Quiz 2

I. Let's review some of the words that you've seen in Groups 11–20. Match each of the following words to the correct definition or synonym on the right. If you need help, refer back to the movie excerpts and definitions. Then check the solutions on page 233.

1. Syntax	A.	Insurrectionists
2. Eulogize	B.	Compendious
3. Insurgents	C.	Dogma
4. Eradicate	D.	Machination
5. Pithy	E.	Filled
6. Revelation	F.	Extol
7. Bevy	G.	Expunge
8. Hermetically	H.	Word arrangement
9. Tactile	I.	Horde
10. Creed	J.	Completely sealed
11. Gambit	K.	Corporeal
12. Replete	L.	Epiphany
13. Interminable	M.	Macabre
14. Dross	N.	Flotsam
15. Gothic	O.	Eternal

II. Let's review several of the word parts that you've seen in Groups 11–20. Match each of the following word parts to the correct definition or synonym on the right. Then check the solutions on page 233.

16. -ics (as in *xenolinguistics*)	A.	Not
17. -logy (as in *morphology*)	B.	Sound
18. Morph- (as in *metamorphosis*)	C.	Study of
19. Phono- (as in *phonology*)	D.	Form
20. In- (as in *interminable*)	E.	Truth
Review from earlier groups:	F.	Study of
21. Veri- (as in *verisimilitude*)		

Quiz 2 (continued)

III. Match each group of synonyms to its general meaning. Then check the solutions on page 233.

22. Formidable Potent Puissant	A. Mixture
23. Agitators Insurgents Insurrectionists Renegades Subversives	B. Loner
24. Amalgamation Composite Fusion Hybrid	C. Short and meaningful
25. Compendious Concise Pithy Succinct Terse	D. Powerful
26. Eremite Hermit Recluse Troglodyte	E. Touchable
27. Corporeal Palpable Tactile Tangible	F. Rebels

Group 21

Here's an excerpt from a movie. See if you can name the movie, describe the scene, and define the boldface vocabulary words. Check your answers on the following page.

SAM: I could do this all day. It comes in waves, these **vivid** symbols. They're symbols, but they're in my mind. You see, all this is in my mind, and Megatron wants what's in my mind . . . him and someone called the Fallen.

JETFIRE: The Fallen? I know him. He left me here to rust! The original Decepticon! He's terrible to work for; it's always **apocalypse, chaos,** crisis. These **transcriptions,** they were part of my mission! The Fallen's search. I remember now! For the Dagger's Tip, and the Key!

Movie: _____

Scene: _____

_____

Vivid might mean _____

_____

Apocalypse might mean _____

_____

Chaos might mean _____

_____

Transcriptions might mean _____

_____

Hint: "I told them to hit the orange smoke . . . It wasn't my best toss, OK?"

Solutions

Let's see how you did. Check your answers and write the exact definitions. To help you memorize the vocabulary words, reread the movie excerpt or even act out the scene with a friend.

Movie: *Transformers: Revenge of the Fallen,* Paramount Pictures, 2009

Scene: After Sam (Shia LaBeouf), Mikaela (Megan Fox), Leo (Ramón Rodríguez), and Agent Simmons (John Turturro) break into the Smithsonian National Air and Space Museum, they find and reactivate Decepticon-turned-Autobot Jetfire. Sam explains the symbols he sees in his mind, and Jetfire transports them all to Egypt.

Inside Scoop: Let's learn some SAT vocabulary from Megan Fox. Regarding fame and Hollywood, she said, "I'm kind of a **recluse**—a hermit. I'm not really out that much because I have a great fear of Hollywood. I think you have to be a really strong human being to survive it, especially if you're a woman." Good word, Megan—*recluse* means *hermit.* You also learned *recluse* as a synonym for *hermit* on *The 40-Year-Old Virgin* movie page (Group 17). Here's one more. Megan has a quote from Shakespeare tattooed on her right shoulder that reads "We will all laugh at **gilded** butterflies." *Gilded* means *covered with gold.* What does this quote mean? Perhaps, just as in the other quote, Megan is expressing a *wariness* (cautiousness) of the Hollywood lifestyle.

Vivid means *bright, clear,* or *lively.*

Apocalypse means *total destruction.* Synonyms: calamity, cataclysm, catastrophe.

Chaos means *disorder.* Synonyms: anarchy, bedlam, mayhem, pandemonium, turmoil.

Transcriptions means *written symbols or words.* This is a great word to break apart. *Trans-* means *across,* as in *transatlantic* (**across** the Atlantic), and *scribe-* means *write,* as in *circumscribe* (**write** around, restrict). So *transcriptions* are *symbols or words* **written across** *mediums,* i.e. from spoken to written or from Sam's mind to the sand where he has written them.

Group 22

Here's an excerpt from a movie. See if you can name the movie, describe the scene, and define the boldface vocabulary words. Check your answers on the following page.

JULES: There's this passage I got memorized: Ezekiel 25:17. "The path of the **righteous** man is **beset** on all sides by the **iniquities** of the selfish and the **tyranny** of evil men. Blessed is he who, in the name of **charity** and **goodwill,** shepherds the weak through the valley of darkness. For he is truly his brother's keeper and the finder of lost children. And I will strike down upon thee with great **vengeance** and furious anger those who attempt to poison and destroy my brothers. And you will know I am the Lord when I lay my vengeance upon you."

Movie: _____

Scene: _____

_____

Righteous might mean _____

Beset might mean _____

Iniquities might mean _____

Tyranny might mean _____

Charity might mean _____

Goodwill might mean _____

Vengeance might mean _____

Hint: Quentin Tarantino won an Academy Award for Best Original Screenplay for this film in 1994.

Solutions

Let's see how you did. Check your answers and write the exact definitions. To help you memorize the vocabulary words, reread the movie excerpt or even act out the scene with a friend.

Movie: *Pulp Fiction,* Miramax Films, 1994

Scene: Jules (Samuel L. Jackson) delivers these lines before he "pops a cap" in someone.

Righteous means *moral* or *honorable*. Synonyms: ethical, scrupulous, upright, virtuous.

Beset means *troubled* or *afflicted*. Synonyms: assailed, bedeviled, beleaguered, besieged, harassed, inundated, oppressed, plagued, tormented.

Iniquities means *sins*. Synonyms for *iniquity:* depravity, impiousness, impropriety, transgression, turpitude, vice, villainy.

Tyranny means *cruel and harsh leadership*. Synonyms: authoritarianism, despotism, Fascism, oppression, subjugation, totalitarianism.

Charity in this case means *kindness*. It can also mean *giving help or money to those in need*. Synonyms: altruism, amity, beneficence, benevolence, caritas, compassion, goodwill, humanity, mercy, munificence, philanthropy, tolerance.

Goodwill means *consideration*. Synonyms: amity, benevolence, charity, collaboration. Antonym: hostility.

Vengeance means *revenge*. Synonyms: reprisal, requital, retaliation, retribution.

Let's translate the boldfaced vocabulary words in the movie excerpt using the definitions provided above:

> "The path of the **honorable** man is **troubled** on all sides by the **sins** of the selfish and the **cruel and harsh leadership** of evil men. Blessed is he who, in the name of **kindness** and **consideration,** shepherds the weak through the valley of darkness . . . And I will strike down upon thee with great **revenge** and furious anger those who attempt to poison and destroy my brothers. And you will know I am the Lord when I lay my revenge upon you."

Group 23

Here's an excerpt from a movie. See if you can name the movie, describe the scene, and define the boldface vocabulary words. Check your answers on the following page.

TYLER: You know why they put oxygen masks on planes?

JACK: So you can breathe.

TYLER: Oxygen . . . gets you high. In a **catastrophic** emergency, you're taking giant, panicked breaths. Suddenly you become **euphoric, docile,** you accept your fate. It's all right here. (*He points to the passive faces of the figures on the Emergency Landing Instruction Card.*) Emergency water landing . . . 600 miles an hour . . . blank faces . . . calm as Hindu cows.

Movie: _____

Scene: _____

_____

Catastrophic might mean _____

_____

Euphoric might mean _____

_____

Docile might mean _____

_____

Hint: Project **Mayhem.**

Solutions

Let's see how you did. Check your answers and write the exact definitions. To help you memorize the vocabulary words, reread the movie excerpt or even act out the scene with a friend.

Movie: *Fight Club,* 20th Century Fox, 1999

Scene: This scene is early in the movie when Edward Norton's character (who never actually has a name, but is sometimes referred to by fans of the film as "Jack") first meets Tyler (Brad Pitt) on the airplane. After this exchange, Tyler has to go to the bathroom, which means he must squeeze past Jack, and he delivers the classic line, "Now a question of **etiquette** . . . as I pass, do I give you the ass or the crotch?" **Etiquette** means *proper or polite behavior.* Synonyms: decorum, propriety, protocol.

Vocabulary in the Hint: *Mayhem* means *disorder* and is a synonym for *anarchy, bedlam, chaos, pandemonium,* and *turmoil.* You learned the word *mayhem* under the *chaos* definition on the *Transformers: Revenge of the Fallen* page (Group 21).

Catastrophic means *disastrous,* like the effects of Tyler's Project Mayhem, which is a group that blows up buildings in order to collapse the United States financial system. Synonyms: apocalyptic, calamitous, cataclysmic.

Euphoric means *blissful.* Synonyms: buoyant, ebullient, ecstatic, elated, exuberant, exultant, jubilant, rapturous.

Docile means *unquestioningly obedient.* Synonyms: acquiescent, amenable, biddable, compliant, deferential, malleable, pliant, submissive, unassertive. Why does Tyler say that Hindu cows are **euphoric** and **docile?** All cows are pretty *docile* (they do what you tell them), but Hindu cows are *euphoric* (blissful) and docile because Hinduism forbids eating cows. That makes Hindu cows much **happier** than, say, Christian or Jewish cows that might get served for dinner.

Group 24

Here are two excerpts from a movie. See if you can name the movie, describe the scenes, and define the boldface vocabulary words. Check your answers on the following page.

KEVIN SANDUSKY: (*speaking quickly in an excited, nerdy way while bushwhacking through the jungle*) You recall that whole **hullabaloo** where Hollywood was split in **schisms,** some studios backing Blu-ray Disc others backing HD DVD. People thought it would come down to pixel rate or refresh rate and they were pretty much the same. What it came down to was a combination of gamers and porn. Now, whichever format porno backs is usually the one that becomes the most successful, but you know Sony . . . every PlayStation 3 has a Blu-ray in it . . .

KIRK LAZARUS: You talking to me this whole time?

––––––––––––

TUGG SPEEDMAN: (*wounded on the battlefield and being rescued by Kirk*) You're my friend. You're my brother . . . but like a really cool brother, ya know . . . like a brother where there was no **animosity.**

KIRK LAZARUS: Don't look now. You've got some real tears going.

TUGG SPEEDMAN: Really?

KIRK LAZARUS: That's the stuff that **accolades** are made of.

Movie: _____

Scenes: _____

Hullabaloo might mean _____

Schisms might mean _____

Animosity might mean _____

Accolades might mean _____

Hint: "Speedman is a dying star. A white dwarf heading for a black hole. That's physics. It's **inevitable.**"

51

Solutions

Let's see how you did. Check your answers and write the exact definitions. To help you memorize the vocabulary words, reread the movie excerpts or even act out the scenes with a friend.

Movie: *Tropic Thunder,* Paramount Pictures, 2008

Scenes: In the first excerpt, the actors have been dropped into the jungle for *candid* (unrehearsed) shots and have split into two groups. In this hilarious scene, Kevin (Jay Baruchel) is passing the time telling the group about HD DVD vs. Blu-ray Disc. In the second excerpt, the actors are escaping the heroin camp (run by the Flaming Dragon gang), but Tugg Speedman (Ben Stiller) is hurt while trying to run away from an explosion, and Kirk (Robert Downey, Jr.) goes back for him. This scene parallels one of the first scenes of the movie, when Tugg could not cry.

Vocabulary in the Hint: *Inevitable* means *unavoidable.* Synonyms: ineludible, inexorable.

Hullabaloo means *commotion.* Synonyms: brouhaha, clamor, furor, fuss, hoo-hah, hubbub, hurly-burly, mayhem, palaver, pandemonium, ruckus, rumpus, to-do, tumult, turmoil.

Schisms means *divided groups based on differences of opinion.* You may have heard this word in history class when you learned about the Great **Schism** of the Middle Ages, in which Christianity **divided** into what later became known as the Eastern Orthodox Church and the Roman Catholic Church. Synonyms for *schism:* breach, break, chasm, disagreement, discord, dissension, gulf, rift, rupture, separation, severance. You might remember the word *chasm* from another terrific Jay Baruchel movie—see if you can *Name That Movie:* "Meanwhile, this Molly is a hard ten, and that five-point **disparity,** that is a **chasm** . . . You can't jump more than two points." Answer: Stainer (T. J. Miller) delivered these lines while analyzing whether Molly (Alice Eve) could possibly be into Kirk (Jay Baruchel) in *She's Out of My League* (Paramount Pictures, 2010).

Animosity means *hatred* or *hostility.* Synonyms: acrimony, antagonism, antipathy, belligerence, enmity, malevolence, malice, rancor, truculence, venom.

Accolades means *honors.* Synonyms: kudos, plaudits.

Group 25

Here are four excerpts from a movie. See if you can name the movie, describe the scenes, and define the boldface vocabulary words. Check your answers on the following page.

ROD: I needed to think about last night. So, I galloped into a wooded **glen,** and after punch-dancing out my rage and suffering an extremely long and very painful fall, I realized what has to be done.

DAVE: There's an ancient Italian **maxim** that roughly translates to "He who is resistant to change is destined to perish."

ROD: Dave, what happened to your eye?

DAVE: This? Is it really noticeable?

ROD: Yeah!

DAVE: Oh, man, it's totally **serendipitous.**

BARRY: I gotta tell you boys, I couldn't be more excited about this jump. When people hear me describing it over the radio, they are going to remember that AM radio is a **viable** and modern source for news and entertainment . . . I've got a tattoo here that fully illustrates my point. It's of this rebellious young man, and he's urinating on an FM radio. And then this other stream of urine is going on to that television set. **Implausible,** I know, but I like to think that . . .

Movie: _____

Scenes: _____

_____

Hint: "My name's Rod. I do awesome stunts all the time with my friends."

Group 25 (continued)

Glen might mean _____

_____

Maxim might mean _____

_____

Serendipitous might mean _____

_____

Viable might mean _____

_____

Implausible might mean _____

_____

Solutions

Let's see how you did. Check your answers and write the exact definitions. To help you memorize the vocabulary words, reread the movie excerpts or even act out the scenes with a friend.

Movie: *Hot Rod,* Paramount Pictures, 2007

Scenes: In the first excerpt, Rod (Andy Samberg) is telling the guys his big plan. In the second, Dave (Bill Hader) and Rico (Danny McBride) are chatting while preparing the pool for breath endurance training. In the third excerpt, Dave is explaining how he hurt his eye. And in the fourth, Barry (Chris Parnell), the AM radio DJ, is talking to Rod and Kevin (Jorma Taccone) before Rod's big jump over fifteen school buses.

Inside Scoop: This script was originally written for Will Ferrell, but Andy Samberg took over the project and added his own touches.

Solutions (continued)

Glen means *valley*.

Maxim means *concise, meaningful statement of truth,* such as Dave's "He who is resistant to change is destined to perish," or the old Klingon proverb, "Revenge is a dish best served cold," shown on the screen at the beginning of *Kill Bill: Volume 1*. Synonyms: adage, aphorism, apothegm, axiom, dictum, epigram, precept, proverb, saw, truism.

Serendipitous means *lucky*. Synonyms: auspicious, felicitous, fortuitous, opportune, propitious.

Viable means *possible*. Synonym: feasible.

Implausible means *unbelievable*.

Group 26

Here are two excerpts from a movie. See if you can name the movie, describe the scenes, and define the boldface vocabulary words. Check your answers on the following page.

SISTER: I understood what he was doing, that he had spent four years fulfilling the **absurd** and **tedious** duty of graduating from college, and now he was **emancipated** from that world of **abstraction,** false security, parents, and **material** excess—the things that cut Chris off from the truth of his existence.

SISTER: I fear for the mother in her—instincts that seem to sense the threat of a loss so huge and **irrevocable** that the mind **balks** at taking its measure.

Movie: _____

Scenes: _____

_____

Absurd might mean _____

Tedious might mean _____

Emancipated might mean _____

Abstraction might mean _____

Material might mean _____

Irrevocable might mean _____

Balks might mean _____

Hint: This movie is based on a true story that originally appeared in *Outside* magazine and was turned into a bestselling book.

Solutions

Let's see how you did. Check your answers and write the exact definitions. To help you memorize the vocabulary words, reread the movie excerpts or even act out the scenes with a friend.

Movie: *Into the Wild,* Paramount Vantage, 2007

Scenes: Chris' (Emile Hirsch) sister, played by Jena Malone, narrates the movie. Luckily for your test scores, she has an excellent vocabulary.

Inside Scoop: Did you notice pre-*Twilight* Kristen Stewart as Tracy, the guitar-playing hippie girl who has a huge crush on Chris? Just don't tell Edward.

Absurd means *unreasonable* or *ridiculous*. Synonyms: farcical, inane, ludicrous, preposterous, risible.

Tedious means *boring*. Synonyms: insipid, lackluster, monochrome, monotonous, mundane, pedestrian, vapid. Antonym: exciting.

Emancipated means *freed,* as in Abraham Lincoln's **Emancipation** Proclamation that **freed** slaves in 1863.

Abstraction means *ideas* or *theories* and comes from the word *abstract,* meaning *conceptual (related to **thoughts**) rather than actual.* Chris was seeking experiences rather than **theories** about experience.

Material in this case means *physical things, such as possessions,* so *material excesses* means *too much stuff.* Synonyms: corporeal, earthly, mundane, physical, secular, tangible, temporal, worldly. Antonym: spiritual.

Irrevocable means *permanent* or *not reversible* since *ir-* means *not* and *revocable* means *reversible*. Synonyms: binding, immutable, incontrovertible, peremptory, unalterable. Antonym: temporary.

Balks means *hesitates*. This is related to a **balk** in baseball, which is called by an umpire when a pitcher **hesitates** during a pitching motion.

Group 27

Here's an excerpt from a movie. See if you can name the movie, describe the scene, and define the boldface vocabulary words. Check your answers on the following page.

DIANE: And now **neglectful** father and Quahog's newest social **pariah,** Peter . . . with another segment of "Grind My Gears." Peter.

PETER: Thank you, Diane. You know what really grinds my gears? People in the nineteenth century. Why don't they get with the friggin' program? It's called an automobile, folks. It's much faster than a horse.

Movie: _____

Scene: _____

_____

Neglectful might mean _____

_____

Pariah might mean _____

_____

Hint: Stewie meets future Stewie.

Solutions

Let's see how you did. Check your answers and write the exact definitions. To help you memorize the vocabulary words, reread the movie excerpt or even act out the scene with a friend.

Movie: *Family Guy Presents Stewie Griffin: The Untold Story,* 20th Century Fox, 2005

Scene: Peter gets a job at the TV station giving a segment, "What Grinds My Gears," on the news, but is fired after Brian and Stewie get drunk and crash the car through the wall of a tavern.

Neglectful means *not caring for properly.* Having an infant who gets drunk and drives into a building is definitely pretty **neglectful.** Synonym: negligent.

Pariah means *outcast.* Synonym: persona non grata. *Persona non grata* is a legal term in international diplomacy. Diplomats have diplomatic immunity. Remember the term *diplomatic immunity* from *Lethal Weapon 2?* If not, how about from the *Family Guy* episode "E. Peterbus Unum," in which Peter raps to MC Hammer's *Can't Touch This:* "Can't touch me / Can't touch me / Ja ja ja ja just like the bad guy / from *Lethal Weapon 2* / I've got **diplomatic immunity**"? Under *diplomatic immunity,* a diplomat cannot be persecuted by the laws of the host nation, but the nation can declare the diplomat a ***persona non grata*** (meaning *an unwelcome person*) and therefore expel him from the country. That ridiculously long explanation is why *persona non grata* is a synonym for *outcast* and *pariah.*

Group 28

Here's an excerpt from a movie. See if you can name the movie, describe the scene, and define the boldface vocabulary words. Check your answers on the following page.

CHEF: (*singing*) Everything worked out, what a happy end. Americans and Canadians are friends again. So, let's all join hands and knock **oppression** down . . .

EVERYONE: Thank God we live in this quiet, little, **pissant**, redneck, **Podunk, jerkwater, greenhorn,** one-horse, mudhole, peckerwood, right-wing, **whistle-stop**, hobnail, truck-driving, old-fashioned, **hayseed**, inbred, **unkempt**, out-of-date, white trash . . . Mountain . . . town!

Movie: _____

Scene: _____

Oppression might mean _____

Pissant might mean _____

Podunk might mean _____

Jerkwater might mean _____

Greenhorn might mean _____

Whistle-stop might mean _____

Hayseed might mean _____

Unkempt might mean _____

Hint: "Look, they killed Kenny!"

Solutions

Let's see how you did. Check your answers and write the exact definitions. To help you memorize the vocabulary words, reread the movie excerpt or even act out the scene with a friend.

Movie: *South Park: Bigger, Longer, & Uncut,* Paramount Pictures, 1999

Scene: This is the song that the whole South Park crew sings at the end of the movie.

Inside Scoop: Pam Brady (not of the *Brady Bunch*) co-wrote this movie and also wrote *Hot Rod*. Now that kinda makes sense!

Oppression means *cruel and unfair use of power.* Synonyms: despotism, persecution, repression, subjection, subjugation, suppression, tyranny. Antonym: freedom.

Pissant means *worthless.* Believe it or not, this derogatory term actually comes from a certain type of ant whose nest smells like urine (because of the ant's venom mixed in with the nesting materials), so the ant is called a piss-ant! Synonym: nugatory.

Podunk refers to *a small, unimportant, and boring town.*

Jerkwater refers to *a small, unimportant, and out-of-the-way town.*

Greenhorn refers to *an inexperienced person.* Synonyms: neophyte, novice, tenderfoot, tyro.

Whistle-stop refers, in this case, to *a small, unimportant town.* It can also refer to *the brief stops of a campaigning politician.*

Hayseed means *a simple, unrefined person from the countryside.* It can also refer literally to *a seed obtained from hay.*

Unkempt means *untidy.*

Aren't you glad we cleared that up? Thanks to Cartman and the gang, you now know way too many words for *small town,* and thanks to Terrance and Phillip, you know every obscenity.

Group 29

Here's an excerpt from a movie. See if you can name the movie, describe the scene, and define the boldface vocabulary words. Check your answers on the following page.

F.B.: I do have a test today . . . It's on European **socialism.** I mean, really, what's the point? I'm not European. I don't plan on being European. So, who gives a crap if they're socialists? They could be **fascist anarchists** and it still wouldn't change the fact that I don't own a car . . . It's not that I **condone** fascism. Or any "**ism**" for that matter.

Movie: _____

Scene: _____

_____

Socialism might mean _____

_____

Fascist might mean _____

_____

Anarchists might mean _____

_____

Condone might mean _____

_____

Ism might mean _____

_____

Hint: "Life moves pretty fast. If you don't stop and look around once in a while, you could miss it."

Solutions

Let's see how you did. Check your answers and write the exact definitions. To help you memorize the vocabulary words, reread the movie excerpt or even act out the scene with a friend.

Movie: *Ferris Bueller's Day Off,* Paramount Pictures, 1986

Scene: Ferris (Matthew Broderick) has convinced his parents that he's too sick to go to school. They agree and have reluctantly gone off to work, leaving him home alone. He is in the shower happily getting ready for his "day off." This movie is a classic and one of the best high-school movies, a must-see. The director, John Hughes, also made the 1980s teen classics *The Breakfast Club, Sixteen Candles,* and *Pretty in Pink!*

Inside Scoop: During the hilarious "Twist and Shout" parade scene, the construction worker and the window washer were not originally part of the film, but were simply dancing to the music being played. John Hughes found them so entertaining that he recorded them and added them to the movie!

Socialism refers to *an economic system in which all people own all property together.*

Fascist describes *an oppressive system of government,* like that of Nazi Germany under Hitler. Synonyms: authoritarian, despotic, dictatorial, draconian, imperious, totalitarian, tyrannical. Antonym: democratic.

Anarchists means *people who believe in total individual freedom and the absence of law.* In fact, *an-* means *without* and *-archy* means *ruler,* so *anarchy* means *without ruler—the absence of law.* The suffix *-archy* helps you remember words like *monarchy* (*mono-* means *one,* so *monarchy* means *rule by one—* usually by a king or queen), *oligarchy* (*oligo-* means *a small number,* so *oligarchy* means *rule by a small group of individuals*), *matriarchy* (*rule by women*), and *plutarchy* (*rule by the wealthy*).

Condone means *reluctantly accept or approve.* Synonym: sanction.

Ism means *philosophy.* You've learned about socialism, fascism, and anarchism. Some other popular isms are feminism, *hedonism* (philosophy that advocates seeking pleasure), and *existentialism* (belief that individuals must find their *own* meaning to existence).

Group 30

Here's an excerpt from a movie. See if you can name the movie, describe the scene, and define the boldface vocabulary words. Check your answers on the following page.

GRACE: Parker, you know, I used to think it was **benign neglect,** but now I see that you're intentionally screwing me . . . I need a researcher, not some jarhead dropout . . .

PARKER: Look, you're supposed to be winning the hearts and the minds of the natives, isn't that the whole point of your little puppet show? . . . Relations with the **indigenous** are only getting worse.

GRACE: Yeah, that tends to happen when you use machine guns on them . . .

Movie: _____

Scene: _____

_____

Benign might mean _____

_____

Neglect might mean _____

_____

Indigenous might mean _____

_____

Hint: "This is why we're here: **Unobtainium** . . . Now those savages are threatening our whole operation. We're on the brink of war, and you're supposed to be finding a **diplomatic** solution."

Solutions

Let's see how you did. Check your answers and write the exact definitions. To help you memorize the vocabulary words, reread the movie excerpt or even act out the scene with a friend.

Movie: *Avatar,* 20th Century Fox, 2009

Scene: Grace (Sigourney Weaver) is angry with Parker (Giovanni Ribisi), who is in charge of the mining operation on the planet Pandora, for assigning Jake Sully (Sam Worthington) to her Avatar Program.

Inside Scoop: The word *avatar* refers to *a god that has taken physical form on Earth.* I think director James Cameron chose this word for the humans who have taken physical form as Na'vi on Pandora in order to demonstrate the humans' arrogance (thinking they are like gods) in their dealings with the Na'vi.

Vocabulary in the Hint: *Unobtainium* is used in science and science fiction to refer to a *fictional (not real) material that is difficult or **impossible** to **obtain**. Un-* means *not,* so **not obtainable**. *Diplomatic* means *dealing with people (or, in this case, the Na'vi who inhabit Pandora) in a sensitive way,* for example, not firing machine guns at them. Synonyms: tactful, suave.

Benign means *kind* or *harmless,* the opposite of *evil* or *harmful.* Synonyms: innocuous, nonmalignant. You hear these words a lot on television doctor shows such as *House, Grey's Anatomy,* and *Scrubs*—a *benign* tumor is *harmless,* and a *malignant* tumor is *cancerous* (*malignant* means *harmful*).

Neglect means *lack of care or attention.* Synonyms: disregard, negligence.

Indigenous means *native* or *home-grown.* Synonyms: aboriginal, autochthonous.

Quiz 3

I. Let's review some of the words that you've seen in Groups 21–30. Match each of the following words to the correct definition or synonym on the right. If you need help, refer back to the movie excerpts and definitions. Then check the solutions on page 233.

1. Apocalypse	A. Amity
2. Iniquity	B. Acquiescent
3. Goodwill	C. Plaudit
4. Euphoric	D. Opportune
5. Docile	E. Inane
6. Schism	F. Catastrophe
7. Animosity	G. Elated
8. Accolade	H. Draconian
9. Maxim	I. Native
10. Serendipitous	J. Turpitude
11. Absurd	K. Chasm
12. Pariah	L. Innocuous
13. Fascist	M. Persona non grata
14. Benign	N. Aphorism
15. Indigenous	O. Acrimony

II. Let's review several of the word parts that you've seen in Groups 21–30. Match each of the following word parts to the correct definition or synonym on the right. Then check the solutions on page 233.

16. Trans- (as in *transcription*)	A. One
17. Ir- (as in *irrevocable*)	B. Sound
18. An- (as in *anarchy*)	C. Not
19. Mono- (as in *monarchy*)	D. Across
20. -archy (as in *anarchy*)	E. Without
Review from earlier groups:	F. Ruler
21. Phono- (as in *phonology*)	

III. Match each group of synonyms to its general meaning. Then check the solutions on page 233.

22. Anarchy
    Bedlam
    Chaos
    Mayhem
    Pandemonium
    Turmoil

    A. Kindness

23. Altruism
    Benevolence
    Caritas
    Charity
    Munificence

    B. Obedient

24. Buoyant
    Ebullient
    Ecstatic
    Elated
    Euphoric
    Exultant
    Jubilant
    Rapturous

    C. Hostility

25. Acquiescent
    Amenable
    Biddable
    Compliant
    Deferential
    Docile
    Malleable
    Pliant
    Submissive

    D. Blissful

26. Acrimony
    Animosity
    Antipathy
    Enmity
    Rancor

    E. Disorder

Group 31

Here's an excerpt from a movie. See if you can name the movie, describe the scene, and define the boldface vocabulary words. Check your answers on the following page.

ARTHUR: It is I, Arthur, son of Uther Pendragon, from the castle of Camelot. King of the Britons, defeater of the Saxons, **sovereign** of all England! . . . And this is my trusty servant, Patsy. We have ridden the length and **breadth** of the land in search of knights who will join me in my court at Camelot . . .

SOLDIER: What, ridden on a horse?

ARTHUR: Yes!

SOLDIER: You're using coconuts! . . . Where'd you get the coconuts?

ARTHUR: We found them.

SOLDIER: Found them? In Mercia? The coconut's **tropical!**

ARTHUR: What do you mean?

SOLDIER: Well, this is a **temperate** zone.

Movie: _____

Scene: _____

_____

Sovereign might mean _____

Breadth might mean _____

Tropical might mean _____

Temperate might mean _____

Hint: "We are the Knights Who Say 'Ni!'"

Solutions

Let's see how you did. Check your answers and write the exact definitions. To help you memorize the vocabulary words, reread the movie excerpt or even act out the scene with a friend.

Movie: *Monty Python and the Holy Grail,* Fox, 1975

Scenes: Early in the movie, Arthur (Graham Chapman) and his trusty servant Patsy (Terry Gilliam) meet the guards at French Castle, who taunt them for using coconuts to simulate the sound of horses' hooves.

Sovereign means *ruler.* That makes sense since *reign* means *rule* as in, "We know you're all robots, and we don't care! Tenacious D! We reign supreme. Oh, God! Burrito supreme, and a chicken supreme, and a cutlass supreme." –JB, *Tenacious D in The Pick of Destiny* (2006). Synonyms: monarch, potentate.

Breadth means *width* and actually comes from the word *broad* (wide).

Tropical means *from the tropics (near the equator).* Technically, it refers to the area on the planet between the Tropic of Cancer and the Tropic of Capricorn. Now, if you ever appear on *Are you Smarter Than a Fifth Grader?,* you'll be prepared!

Temperate means *mild.* Synonym: clement. In a related use, *temperate* can also mean *restrained* or **mild**-*mannered,* and *temper* can mean *counterbalance* or *soften.* Standardized tests love to test those alternate meanings, but the guard in this movie simply meant that coconuts grow in hot places, not mild climates.

Group 32

Here are three excerpts from a movie. See if you can name the movie, describe the scenes, and define the boldface vocabulary words. Check your answers on the following page.

VERONICA: Mr. Burgundy, you are acting like a baby.

RON: I'm not a baby, I am a man. I am an anchorman.

VERONICA: You are not a man. You are a big, fat joke.

RON: I'm a man who discovered the wheel and built the Eiffel Tower out of metal and **brawn.** That's what kind of man I am.

RON: Oh, you woke the bears. Why did you do that? . . . It took my **impending** death for me to realize how much I need you.

VERONICA: Oh, Ron.

WES MANTOOTH: Today we spell "**redemption**" . . . R-O-N.

Movie: _____

Scenes: _____

_____

Brawn might mean _____

_____

Impending might mean _____

_____

Redemption might mean _____

_____

Hint: "It's so damn hot. Milk was a bad choice."

Solutions

Let's see how you did. Check your answers and write the exact definitions. To help you memorize the vocabulary words, reread the movie excerpts or even act out the scenes with a friend.

Movie: *Anchorman: The Legend of Ron Burgundy,* DreamWorks, 2004

Scenes: In the first excerpt, Ron (Will Ferrell) and Veronica (Christina Applegate) are arguing. In the second excerpt, Ron has jumped into the bear pit to save Veronica, and in the third excerpt, Ron has saved the day, and Ron's rival, Wes Mantooth (brilliantly played by Vince Vaughn), declares Ron the hero of the day. Here's a little vocab extra: During the bear fight Ron says, "Hit him in the uvula!" Anyone know what a *uvula* is? It's that fleshy thing dangling in the back of your throat.

Inside Scoop: Did you catch Seth Rogen in one of his first movie appearances as the "eager cameraman" filming Veronica's story at the cat fashion show and later at the zoo? Jack Black also cameos as the irate motorcyclist who punts Ron's dog, Baxter, off the bridge. I wonder if Jack Black caused the popularity of "broseph" and "that's how I roll" when he used them in this movie.

Brawn means *physical strength.*

Impending means *looming* or *coming soon.* The SAT and ACT love this word and its synonyms, *forthcoming* and *imminent.*

Redemption means *forgiveness for or salvation from sin.* Synonym: absolution.

Group 33

Here's an excerpt from a movie. See if you can name the movie, describe the scene, and define the boldface vocabulary word. Check your answers on the following page.

HORACE: Don't think I don't know why you're here, Albus. The answer is still no. Absolutely and **unequivocally** no.

Movie: _____

Scene: _____

_____

Unequivocally might mean _____

_____

Hint: "Lumos!"

Solutions

Let's see how you did. Check your answers and write the exact definition. To help you memorize the vocabulary word, reread the movie excerpt or even act out the scene with a friend.

Movie: *Harry Potter and the Half-Blood Prince,* Warner Bros., 2009

Scene: At the beginning of the movie, Albus Dumbledore (Michael Gambon) steals Harry Potter (Daniel Radcliffe) away from a hot date in order to find Horace Slughorn (Jim Broadbent). Dumbledore knows that Slughorn will take an interest in Harry and plans for Harry to retrieve a crucial memory from Slughorn.

Vocabulary in the Hint: *Lumos* is a magical spell for light; basically, it turns the spell caster's wand into a flashlight. *Lumos* comes from *lumin-*, meaning *light,* as in *luminous* (radiant) and *luminary* (a person who en**light**ens and inspires others).

Unequivocally means *definitely*. What does *unequivocal* have to do with being **definite?** *Equiv-* means *equal,* and *vocal* refers to *expressing,* so *unequivocally* means *not expressing (options) as equal,* that is, *being sure—**definite.** Synonyms: categorically, incontrovertibly, indubitably, unconditionally, unqualifiedly. All of these synonyms show up very frequently on standardized tests. Remember to say or write every new vocabulary word and its synonyms five times—it's a great way to memorize a bunch of new words all at one time.

Group 34

Here's an excerpt from a movie. See if you can name the movie, describe the scene, and define the boldface vocabulary words. Check your answers on the following page.

UHURA: Was I not one of your top students?

SPOCK: Indeed you were.

UHURA: And did I not, on multiple occasions, demonstrate an exceptional **aural** sensitivity and . . . I quote . . . "an **unparalleled** ability to identify **sonic anomalies** in subspace transmissions tests?"

SPOCK: Consistently, yes.

UHURA: And while you were well aware of my **unqualified** desires to serve aboard the . . .

Movie: _____

Scene: _____

_____

Aural might mean _____

Unparalleled might mean _____

Sonic might mean _____

Anomalies might mean _____

Unqualified might mean _____

Hint: "You have failed to **divine** the purpose of the test (the Kobayashi Maru no-win scenario)."

Solutions

Let's see how you did. Check your answers and write the exact definitions. To help you memorize the vocabulary words, reread the movie excerpt or even act out the scene with a friend.

Movie: *Star Trek,* Paramount Pictures, 2009

Scene: The cadets have just received their assignments from Starfleet. Uhura is Spock's girlfriend, and she's angry that Spock (who is her superior officer) assigned her to the USS *Farrigat* rather than the USS *Enterprise.* Who knew that young Spock was such a player? The score is Kirk 0, Spock 1.

Inside Scoop: Did you recognize Tyler Perry as Admiral Barnett from Kirk's Disciplinary Hearing? This was Perry's first movie role outside of his own films, such as *Madea Goes to Jail.*

Vocabulary in the Hint: *Divine* means *discover* or *predict* and comes from the Latin *divus* meaning *godlike,* since gods can **discover** and **predict** everything. The related word *divination* means *predicting the future by supernatural means,* as in Harry Potter's least favorite class, Divination, taught by Professor Sybill Trelawney. Harry's opinion of the class is no doubt influenced by Trelawney's frequent predictions of Harry's *imminent* (looming) demise.

Aural means *relating to the ear.* Oddly, the word for *relating to the mouth,* which is *oral,* sounds almost exactly the same when pronounced.

Unparalleled means *having no parallel or equal.* You might remember from Geometry class that **parallel** lines run **alongside** each other and have **equal** slopes. Something that is unparalleled is exceptional and has no equal. Synonyms: elite, exceptional, nonpareil, singular, unprecedented.

Sonic means *relating to sound,* as in Sega's **Sonic** the Hedgehog, who can run faster than the speed of **sound.**

Anomalies means *irregularities* or *abnormalities.* Since *a-* means *not, anomalies* even sounds a bit like *not normal.* Synonym: aberrations.

Unqualified in this case means *absolute.* Synonyms: categorical, unconditional, unequivocal, unmitigated, untempered. *Unqualified* can, of course, also mean *untrained* or *unable.*

Group 35

Here's an excerpt from a movie. See if you can name the movie, describe the scene, and define the boldface vocabulary word. Check your answers on the following page.

SARAH LIVINGSTON: . . . various scams going on. One of them was the cat-food scam, where they sold cat food to the aliens for **exorbitant** prices.

Movie: _____

Scene: _____

_____

Exorbitant might mean _____

_____

Hint: "The **derogatory** term 'prawn' is used for the alien."

Solutions

Let's see how you did. Check your answers and write the exact definition. To help you memorize the vocabulary word, reread the movie excerpt or even act out the scene with a friend.

Movie: *District 9,* TriStar Pictures, 2009

Scene: Early in the film, a sociologist named Sarah Livingston (Nathalie Boltt) describes the conditions in District 9. She explains that organized crime within the district is selling cat food to the extraterrestrial aliens. A journalist explains that the aliens love cat food; it's like "catnip for cats, only a lot more intense."

Inside Scoop: *District 9* was written and directed by Neill Blomkamp, who based the film on his observations of *apartheid* (policy of segregation based on race) while growing up in South Africa.

Vocabulary in the Hint: *Derogatory* means *disrespectfully critical.* Synonyms: defamatory, denigrating, deprecating, depreciatory, disparaging, pejorative.

Exorbitant means *unfairly high.* This is an interesting word to break apart. *Ex-* means *out,* as in *extricate* (*get* **out**; the South African government, with the help of the private military company MNU, is trying to **extricate** the aliens from District 9), and *orbit* means *track,* as in the Earth's **orbit** abound the sun. So, *exorbitant* literally translates as *out of track,* like the prices are way **out of track**—*way too high.* Synonym: extortionate.

Group 36

Here are three excerpts from a movie. See if you can name the movie, describe the scenes, and define the boldface vocabulary words. Check your answers on the following page.

THOMAS GATES: It's a playfair **cipher.**

JOHN WILKES BOOTH: Can you decode it?

_____

BEN GATES: Dr. Samuel Mudd was convicted of being a co-**conspirator** in the Lincoln assassination. The evidence was **circumstantial.** He was later **pardoned,** but it didn't matter. Mudd's name still lives in **infamy,** and I will not let Thomas Gates' name be mud.

_____

BEN GATES: You can give that history back to its **descendants.** And because you're the President of the United States, sir, whether by **innate** character or . . .

Movie: _____

Scenes: _____

Cipher might mean _____

Conspirator might mean _____

Circumstantial might mean _____

Pardoned might mean _____

Infamy might mean _____

Descendants might mean _____

Innate might mean _____

Hint: "Of course, someone else is after the treasure. It's the **axiom** of treasure hunting."

Solutions

Let's see how you did. Check your answers and write the exact definitions. To help you memorize the vocabulary words, reread the movie excerpts or even act out the scenes with a friend.

Movie: *National Treasure: Book of Secrets,* Walt Disney Pictures, 2007

Scenes: Ben (Nicolas Cage) and Riley (Justin Bartha) are hot on the trail of another treasure. This time it's the Lost City of Gold. In the first excerpt, Thomas Gates decodes a cipher for Booth. In the second, Ben explains why he must pursue the treasure and clear the Gates name. In the third excerpt, Ben asks for help from the President of the United States (Bruce Greenwood).

Inside Scoop: Did you recognize Justin Bartha (who plays Riley Poole) as the missing groom, Doug Billings, from *The Hangover?*

Vocabulary in the Hint: *Axiom* means *accepted truth.* Synonyms: adage, aphorism, apothegm, dictum, gnome (not to be confused with small, bearded, garden-statue gnomes), maxim, principle, truism.

Cipher means *code.* That's why *decipher* means *decode.* Synonym: cryptogram.

Conspirator comes from *conspire* and describes *a person who makes secret plans with another.*

Circumstantial means *indirect,* and literally comes from the word *circumstance.* It refers to evidence that the **circumstances** imply but do not prove.

Pardoned means *freed of blame* and is the opposite of *condemned.* Synonyms: absolved, acquitted, exculpated, exonerated, vindicated. You hear some of these words in crime dramas like *CSI* and *NCIS.*

Infamy means *fame for something bad,* as in Franklin Roosevelt's famous speech after the attack on Pearl Harbor in which he described that day as "a date which will live in infamy."

Descendants means *relatives that come after.* The opposite of *descendants* is *ancestors* (relatives that came before).

Innate means *present from birth* or *natural.* Synonyms: connate, inborn, inherent, instinctive, intrinsic.

Group 37

Here's an excerpt from a movie. See if you can name the movie, describe the scene, and define the boldface vocabulary words. Check your answers on the following page.

PIPPIN: Here do I swear **fealty** and service to Gondor, in peace or war, in living or dying, from this hour henceforth, until my lord release me . . . or death take me.

DENETHOR: And I shall not forget it, nor fail to reward that which is given: Fealty with love, **valor** with honor, disloyalty with **vengeance**.

Movie: _____

Scene: _____

_____

Fealty might mean _____

_____

Valor might mean _____

_____

Vengeance might mean _____

_____

Hint: "You think you are wise, Mithrandir. Yet for all your **subtleties,** you have not wisdom. Do you think the eyes of the White Tower are blind? I have seen more than you know. With your left hand you would use me as a shield against Mordor, and with your right you would seek to **supplant** me. I know who rides with Theoden of Rohan. Oh, yes. Word has reached my ears of this Aragorn, son of Arathorn, and I tell you now, I will not bow to this Ranger from the North, last of a ragged house long **bereft of** lordship!"

Solutions

Let's see how you did. Check your answers and write the exact definitions. To help you memorize the vocabulary words, reread the movie excerpt or even act out the scene with a friend.

Movie: *The Lord of the Rings: The Return of the King,* New Line Cinema, 2003

Scene: Pippin (Billy Boyd) swears allegiance to Denethor (John Noble), Steward of Gondor.

Vocabulary in the Hint: *Subtleties* in this case means *clever methods of achieving something.* Synonyms for *subtlety:* canniness, percipience, perspicacity, shrewdness. *Subtleties* can also mean *small or understated distinctions between things,* like in the subtle flavors of expensive wine. *Supplant* means *replace, usually by force.* Synonyms: displace, supersede, usurp. *Bereft of* means *lacking.* Synonym: sans.

Fealty means *loyalty.* Synonym: fidelity.

Valor means *bravery.* Synonyms: audacity, courage, dauntlessness, gallantry, moxie, pluck. Antonym: cowardice.

Vengeance means *revenge.* Synonyms: reprisal, requital, retaliation, retribution.

Group 38

Here's an excerpt from a movie. See if you can name the movie, describe the scene, and define the boldface vocabulary words. Check your answers on the following page.

B: Beautiful, isn't it?

Lucius Fox: Beautiful. **Unethical.** *Dangerous.* You've turned every cell phone . . . into a microphone.

B: And a high-frequency generator-receiver.

Lucius Fox: You took my **sonar** concept and applied it to every phone in the city. . . . This is wrong.

B: I've gotta find this man, Lucius.

Lucius Fox: At what cost?

B: The database is null-key **encrypted.** It can only be accessed by one person.

Lucius Fox: This is too much power for one person.

Movie: _____

Scene: _____

_____

Unethical might mean _____

Sonar might mean _____

Encrypted might mean _____

Hint: "In China, Lau Security Investments stands for **dynamic** new growth. A joint Chinese venture with Wayne Enterprises will be a powerhouse."

Solutions

Let's see how you did. Check your answers and write the exact definitions. To help you memorize the vocabulary words, reread the movie excerpt or even act out the scene with a friend.

Movie: *The Dark Knight,* Warner Bros., 2008

Scene: Batman (Christian Bale) shows Lucius (Morgan Freeman) the machine he built to locate the Joker (Heath Ledger).

Vocabulary in the Hint: *Dynamic* means *changing, energetic,* or *bold.*

Unethical means *not moral.*

Sonar means *the system of using sound to locate objects in one's environment.* The name *sonar* comes from **SO**und **NA**vigation and **R**anging, that is, using sound to locate objects in one's environment in order to navigate among them.

Encrypted means *coded to keep secret* and comes from *crypt-* meaning *hidden.* The type of encryption, "null-key," mentioned in the movie excerpt actually exists and is a non-invasive, but powerful form of encryption. Synonym: ciphered.

Group 39

Here's an excerpt from a movie. See if you can name the movie, describe the scene, and define the boldface vocabulary words. Check your answers on the following page.

CASSIUS: On this day, we reach back to **hallowed antiquity,** to bring you a re-creation of the second fall of mighty Carthage! . . . On the **barren** plain of Zama, there stood the **invincible** armies of the barbarian Hannibal. **Ferocious mercenaries** and warriors from all **brute** nations, bent on **merciless** destruction, conquest. Your emperor is pleased to give you the barbarian **horde!** (*Crowd cheers.*)

Movie: _____

Scene: _____

_____

Hallowed might mean _____

Antiquity might mean _____

Barren might mean _____

Invincible might mean _____

Ferocious might mean _____

Mercenaries might mean _____

Brute might mean _____

Merciless might mean _____

Horde might mean _____

Hint: "What we do in life echoes in eternity!"

Solutions

Let's see how you did. Check your answers and write the exact definitions. To help you memorize the vocabulary words, reread the movie excerpt or even act out the scene with a friend.

Movie: *Gladiator,* DreamWorks, 2000

Scene: What a great scene; it gives me chills every time! This excerpt is of the announcer giving the introduction before Maximus' (Russell Crowe) first fight as a gladiator in the Roman Coliseum. The barbarian horde is expected to lose to the chariots of Scipio Africanus, but Maximus organizes the gladiators into staggered columns, instructs them to lock shields, and switches to a diamond formation to overturn a chariot. He then divides them into single columns to pursue and defeat the chariots, a massive underdog victory.

Hallowed means *sacred*. Synonyms: consecrated, inviolable, sacrosanct, sanctified.

Antiquity means *the ancient past*. That's easy to remember since *antiquity* sounds like *antique* (a collectable item from the **past**), such as the dusty candy dish that your grandma doesn't let you touch. The Battle of Zama occurred 400 years before the events depicted in *Gladiator*, so to the crowd watching the re-creation of the battle in the Roman Coliseum, the battle really was **ancient** history, the same way Galileo's lifetime might seem to you.

Barren means *empty, bleak,* or *lifeless*. Synonyms: desolate, infecund, infertile, sterile.

Invincible means *undefeatable*. Synonyms: impregnable, incontrovertible, indomitable, inviolable, unassailable.

Ferocious means *fierce*. Synonyms: feral, savage, undomesticated.

Mercenaries means *hired soldiers*. Synonym: condottiere.

Brute means *crude or violent*.

Merciless means *pitiless*. Synonyms: callous, heartless, ruthless.

Horde means *mob*. Synonym: throng.

Group 40

Here's an excerpt from a movie. See if you can name the movie, describe the scene, and define the boldface vocabulary words. Check your answers on the following page.

BRIAN: Time to musk up. (*opens his hidden chamber of colognes*)

RON: Wow. Never ceases to amaze me. What cologne you gonna go with? London Gentleman, or wait . . . no, no, no, hold on, Blackbeard's Delight?

BRIAN: No, she gets a special cologne . . . It's called Sex Panther, by Odeon. It's illegal in nine countries . . . Yep, it's made with bits of real panther, so you know it's good.

RON: It's quite **pungent.**

BRIAN: Oh, yeah.

RON: It's a **formidable** scent . . . It stings the nostrils. In a good way.

BRIAN: Yep.

RON: Brian, I'm gonna be honest with you. That smells like pure gasoline.

BRIAN: They've done studies, you know. Sixty percent of the time, it works every time.

RON: That doesn't make sense.

Movie: _____

Scene: _____

_____

Pungent might mean _____

Formidable might mean _____

Hint: "Everyone just relax, all right? Believe me, if there's one thing Ron Burgundy knows, it's women."

Solutions

Let's see how you did. Check your answers and write the exact definitions. To help you memorize the vocabulary words, reread the movie excerpt or even act out the scene with a friend.

Movie: *Anchorman: The Legend of Ron Burgundy,* DreamWorks, 2004

Scene: Brian (Paul Rudd) is *musking up* (putting on cologne) before setting out to "hit on" Veronica (Christina Applegate). He has a secret cabinet where he keeps his extensive supply of colognes. When Brian enters the newsroom, everyone is appalled by the scent.

Inside Scoop: Judd Apatow, perhaps the king of modern comedy, produced this movie and makes a cameo as the man in the newsroom who says that Brian's cologne smells like, "A turd covered in burnt hair." Apatow is also responsible for *Knocked Up, The 40-Year-Old Virgin, Superbad, Talladega Nights, Step Brothers,* and *Forgetting Sarah Marshall!*

Pungent means *strong* or *sharp*. Synonyms: acerbic, acrimonious, biting, caustic, incisive, sarcastic, sardonic, scathing, trenchant, venomous.

Formidable means *powerful* or *intimidating*. The cologne's scent is so **powerful** that everyone flees the newsroom, and Brian has to be scrubbed down and doused with a fire hose. Synonym: puissant.

Quiz 4

I. Let's review some of the words that you've seen in Groups 31–40. Match each of the following words to the correct definition or synonym on the right. If you need help, refer back to the movie excerpts and definitions. Then check the solutions on page 233.

1. Sovereign	A. Imminent
2. Impending	B. Aberration
3. Unequivocal	C. Extortionate
4. Anomaly	D. Maxim
5. Derogatory	E. Fidelity
6. Exorbitant	F. Potentate
7. Axiom	G. Puissant
8. Infamy	H. Categorical
9. Innate	I. Callous
10. Fealty	J. Trenchant
11. Pardoned	K. Pejorative
12. Hallowed	L. Exculpated
13. Merciless	M. Fame for something bad
14. Pungent	N. Sacrosanct
15. Formidable	O. Intrinsic

II. Let's review several of the word parts that you've seen in Groups 31–40. Match each of the following word parts to the correct definition or synonym on the right. Then check the solutions on page 233.

16. Lumin- (as in *luminous*)	A. Out
17. Equiv- (as in *equivocal*)	B. Godlike
18. A- (as in *anomaly*)	C. Hidden
19. Divus (as in *divination*)	D. Light
20. Ex- (as in *extricate*)	E. Equal
21. Crypt- (as in *encrypted*)	F. Not

Quiz 4 (continued)

III. Match each group of synonyms to its general meaning. Then check the solutions on page 233.

22. Forthcoming Imminent Impending	A. Disrespectfully critical
23. Categorical Incontrovertible Indubitable Unconditional Unequivocal Unqualified	B. Accepted truth
24. Defamatory Depreciatory Derogatory Disparaging Pejorative	C. Looming
25. Adage Aphorism Apothegm Axiom Dictum Gnome Maxim Truism	D. Freed of blame
26. Absolved Acquitted Exculpated Exonerated Pardoned Vindicated	E. Definite

Group 41

Here are two excerpts from a movie. See if you can name the movie, describe the scenes, and define the boldface vocabulary words. Check your answers on the following page.

RA'S AL GHUL: Only a **cynical** man would call what these people have "lives," Wayne. Crime, despair . . . this is not how man was supposed to live. The League of Shadows has been a check against human corruption for thousands of years. We sacked Rome, loaded trade ships with plague rats, burned London to the ground. Every time a civilization reaches the **pinnacle** of its **decadence,** we return to restore the balance.

———————

BRUCE: To all of you, uh . . . all you phonies, all of you two-faced friends, you **sycophantic** suck-ups who smile through your teeth at me, please leave me in peace. Please go. Stop smiling. It's not a joke. Please leave. The party's over. Get out.

Movie: _____

Scenes: _____

_____

Cynical might mean _____

_____

Pinnacle might mean _____

_____

Decadence might mean _____

_____

Sycophantic might mean _____

_____

Hint: At the very end of this movie, you are briefly introduced to the character that Heath Ledger plays in the sequel.

Solutions

Let's see how you did. Check your answers and write the exact definitions. To help you memorize the vocabulary words, reread the movie excerpts or even act out the scenes with a friend.

Movie: *Batman Begins,* Warner Bros., 2005

Scenes: Ra's al Ghul (Liam Neeson) is explaining to Bruce Wayne (Christian Bale) why he does what he does. This is the villain-tells-all scene in every superhero movie. In the second quote, Bruce is telling the guests to leave his birthday party at the Wayne mansion. He is speaking harshly so that the guests will leave quickly; he wants them out of the house so that they will not get hurt from the fight that he knows will ensue between himself and Ra's al Ghul's *lackeys* (followers).

Cynical means *distrusting the motives of others*. Synonyms: dubious, skeptical.

Pinnacle means *highest point*. Synonyms: acme, apex, apogee, capstone, crest, peak, summit, zenith. Antonym: nadir.

Decadence means *excessive self-indulgence*. Synonyms: debauchery, degeneracy, depravity, hedonism, immoderateness, intemperance, licentiousness, vice.

Sycophantic means *flattering to get something from someone of power*. Basically, Bruce defines the word for you right after he says it—a sycophantic person is a "suck-up." A sycophantic person acts in an obsequious, oleaginous, servile, or toady (all four of these excellent vocabulary words mean *overly submissive*) way and flatters excessively to get what he or she wants.

Group 42

Here's an excerpt from a movie. See if you can name the movie, describe the scene, and define the boldface vocabulary words. Check your answers on the following page.

SMITH: Illusions, Mr. Anderson . . . **vagaries** of perception. The temporary **constructs** of a **feeble** human intellect trying desperately to justify an existence that is without meaning or purpose. And all of them as **artificial** as the Matrix itself, although only a human mind could invent something as **insipid** as love. You must be able to see it, Mr. Anderson. You must know it by now. You can't win. It's pointless to keep fighting. Why, Mr. Anderson? Why? Why do you persist?

Movie: _____

Scene: _____

_____

Vagaries might mean _____

_____

Constructs might mean _____

_____

Feeble might mean _____

_____

Artificial might mean _____

_____

Insipid might mean _____

_____

Hint: Would you choose the red pill or the blue pill?

Solutions

Let's see how you did. Check your answers and write the exact definitions. To help you memorize the vocabulary words, reread the movie excerpt or even act out the scene with a friend.

Movie: *The Matrix: Revolutions,* Warner Bros., 2003

Scene: Neo (Keanu Reeves) and Agent Smith (Hugo Weaving) have been duking it out in a crazy fight sequence. At every break in the action, Smith goes into one of his maniacal monologues. The fight ends with Smith taking over Neo, and then Neo deprogramming Smith.

Vagaries means *unexpected changes*. This comes from the Latin word *vagari,* which means *wander,* as in a *vagrant* (a homeless person who **wanders**). Synonyms: caprice, eccentricities, fluctuations, foibles, peculiarities, quirks, whimsy.

Constructs means *theories, usually created without much solid evidence*. It comes from the word *construct—to build* the theory. The word *construct* is just *con-,* which means *with,* just like in Spanish, and *-struct,* which refers to *structure.*

Feeble means *very weak*. Synonyms: frail, impuissant.

Artificial means *fake,* or more specifically *human-made rather than naturally occurring,* like artificial flavors. Interestingly, *artifice* means *trickery,* like tricking someone into thinking that something tastes like watermelon when it is really a synthetic chemical. Synonyms: bogus, contrived, ersatz, fabricated, faux, feigned, inorganic, mock, spurious, synthetic. Crossword puzzles love to use the word *ersatz,* and standardized tests love *spurious.*

Insipid means *lacking flavor or spirit*. Synonyms: banal, flat, hackneyed, inane, jejune, pedestrian, tired, trite, vapid.

Group 43

Here's an excerpt from a movie. See if you can name the movie, describe the scene, and define the boldface vocabulary words. Check your answers on the following page.

Voilà! In view, a humble **vaudevillian** veteran, cast **vicariously** as both victim and villain by the **vicissitudes** of Fate. This **visage,** no mere **veneer** of **vanity,** is a **vestige** of the *vox populi,* now vacant, vanished. However, this **valorous** visitation of a bygone **vexation** stands **vivified** and has vowed to **vanquish** these **venal** and **virulent** vermin **vanguarding vice** and **vouchsafing** the violently vicious and **voracious** violation of **volition.**

Movie: _____

Scene: _____

_____

Vaudevillian might mean _____

Vicariously might mean _____

Vicissitudes might mean _____

Visage might mean _____

Veneer might mean _____

Vanity might mean _____

Vestige might mean _____

Vox populi might mean _____

Valorous might mean _____

Hint: All the "V" words should give this one away.

Group 43 (continued)

Vexation might mean _____

Vivified might mean _____

Vanquish might mean _____

Venal might mean _____

Virulent might mean _____

Vanguarding might mean _____

Vice might mean _____

Vouchsafing might mean _____

Voracious might mean _____

Volition might mean _____

Solutions

Let's see how you did. Check your answers and write the exact definitions. To help you memorize the vocabulary words, reread the movie excerpt or even act out the scene with a friend.

Movie: *V for Vendetta*, Warner Bros., 2006

Scene: V meets Evey (Natalie Portman) and gives his famous introduction containing a vast verbiage of "V" words.

Inside Scoop: Do you recognize V's voice? V is played by Hugo Weaving, the same actor who plays Agent Smith in the *Matrix* movies, Elrond in the *Lord of the Rings* movies, and Megatron in the *Transformers* movies!

Vaudevillian means *relating to entertainment variety shows from the 1920s that were called "vaudeville."*

Vicariously in this case means *instead of another*. It can also mean *experiencing something through someone else.*

Vicissitudes means *changes, usually for the worse.*

Visage means *face.*

Veneer means *fake surface.*

Vanity means *pride or egotism.*

Vestige means *remainder.*

Vox populi translates as *voice of the people* in Latin and refers to *popular opinion.*

Valorous means *brave.*

Vexation means *frustration, annoyance, or worry.*

Vivified means *enlivened.*

Vanquish means *defeat.*

Venal means *corrupt.*

Virulent means *hostile.*

Vanguarding means *promoting.*

Vice means *wickedness.*

Vouchsafing means *revealing* or *granting.*

Voracious means *greedy.*

Volition means *will.*

Let's translate V's *verbiage* (wordiness) now that you have definitions:

> **V:** *Voilà!* In view, a humble **theater** veteran, cast **instead of another** as both victim and villain by the **changes** of Fate. This **face,** no mere **fake surface** of **pride,** is a **remainder** of the **voice of the people,** now vacant, vanished. However, this **brave** visitation of a bygone **annoyance** stands **enlivened** and has vowed to **defeat** these **corrupt** and **hostile** vermin **promoting wickedness** and **revealing** the violently vicious and **greedy** violation of **will.**

Whew! That makes more sense!

Group 44

Here's an excerpt from a movie. See if you can name the movie, describe the scene, and define the boldface vocabulary words. Check your answers on the following page.

D.E.: No, actually the boy is quite **astute.** I really am trying to kill him, but so far unsuccessfully. He's quite **wily,** like his old man.

Movie: _____

Scene: _____

_____

Astute might mean _____

_____

Wily might mean _____

_____

Hint: "Yeah baby, yeah!"

Solutions

Let's see how you did. Check your answers and write the exact definitions. To help you memorize the vocabulary words, reread the movie excerpt or even act out the scene with a friend.

Movie: *Austin Powers: International Man of Mystery,* New Line Cinema, 1997

Scene: Dr. Evil (Mike Myers) and his son, Scott Evil (Seth Green), are in group therapy together. Scott tells the group that his dad wants to kill him. The therapist reassures him that "We might say that [we want to kill each other] sometimes, but we really don't." But Dr. Evil corrects her, saying "No, actually the boy is quite astute. I really am trying to kill him, but so far unsuccessfully. He's quite wily, like his old man."

Inside Scoop: The therapist is played by Carrie Fisher, who played Princess Leia in *Star Wars!*

Astute means *intelligent and insightful*. Synonyms: canny, incisive, judicious, keen, perspicacious, sagacious, savvy, shrewd, wise. *Keen* can also mean *eager*.

Wily means *clever and devious*. Synonyms: artful, calculating, crafty, cunning, foxy (which can also mean *sexy*, but probably not on the SATs), machinating, scheming, sly.

Group 45

Here are three excerpts from a movie. See if you can name the movie, describe the scenes, and define the boldface vocabulary words. Check your answers on the following page.

JEFFREY: I just want to understand this, sir. Every time a rug is **micturated** upon in this fair city, I have to **compensate** the person?

———————

THE DUDE: Let me explain something to you. Um . . . I am not Mr. Lebowski. *You're* Mr. Lebowski. I'm the Dude. So that's what you call me. You know, that or His Dudeness, or Duder, or El Duderino if you're not into the whole **brevity** thing.

———————

MAUDE: Don't be **fatuous**, Jeffrey.

Movie: _____

Scenes: _____

_____

Micturated might mean _____

_____

Compensate might mean _____

_____

Brevity might mean _____

_____

Fatuous might mean _____

_____

Hint: "The Dude **abides**."

Solutions

Let's see how you did. Check your answers and write the exact definitions. To help you memorize the vocabulary words, reread the movie excerpts or even act out the scenes with a friend.

Movie: *The Big Lebowski,* PolyGram Films, 1998

Scenes: In the first two quotes, the Dude is asking Jeffrey Lebowski to replace his rug. In the third excerpt, the Dude meets Jeffrey's daughter, Maude, a wacky *avant-garde* (innovative) artist.

Vocabulary in the Hint: "The Dude **abides**" means "The Dude **obeys**," which is ironic since the Dude does his own thing and does not **obey** anyone. This statement, though, was in response, at the end of the movie, to the narrator's comment "Take it easy," to which the Dude replies, "The Dude abides." That's true; the Dude takes life slow and easy. *Abide* can also mean *tolerate,* which also makes sense since the Dude is pretty **tolerant,** unless, of course, you urinate on his rug.

Micturated means *urinated.* Believe it or not, another equally fancy term for peeing is *emiction.* So you can pee, urinate, micturate, or even emictate, just don't do it on the Dude's rug!

Compensate means *pay back* or *make up for.* Synonyms: atone, expiate, indemnify, make amends, make reparation, recompense, rectify, remunerate, requite.

Brevity means *briefness.* Shakespeare said, "Brevity is the soul of wit," meaning if you want to be funny, keep it short. The opposite of *brevity* is *verbosity* (wordiness, long-windedness).

Fatuous means *silly* or *foolish.* Synonyms: absurd, asinine, inane, vacuous, vapid.

Group 46

Here's an excerpt from a movie. See if you can name the movie, describe the scene, and define the boldface vocabulary words. Check your answers on the following page.

STU: (*meekly raising his hand*) I got a question. Um, you said, "When your shift ended." Does that means you're a nurse, or a black jack dealer . . . ?

JADE: You know this . . . I'm a stripper. Well . . . *technically* I'm an **escort,** but stripping's a great way to meet the clients.

PHIL: Smart.

STU: Savvy.

JADE: But, that's all in the past now that I married a doctor.

STU: I'm just a dentist.

Movie: _____

Scene: _____

_____

Escort might mean _____

_____

Savvy might mean _____

_____

Hint: "Eew! Alan, did you just eat sofa pizza?"

Solutions

Let's see how you did. Check your answers and write the exact definitions. To help you memorize the vocabulary words, reread the movie excerpt or even act out the scene with a friend.

Movie: *The Hangover,* Warner Bros., 2009

Scene: The guys find Jade (Stu's new wife, played by Heather Graham), who fills in lots of missing info, but they still don't know where to find their friend, Doug (Justin Bartha), who is supposed to get married later in the day.

Inside Scoop: Here's a *Hangover* trivia question for you. You know who left the baby, why Stu's (Ed Helms) tooth is missing, and how the tiger got into the bathroom, but why is a live chicken walking around the room? Answer: Director Todd Phillips says that the guys were planning on feeding the chicken to the tiger.

Escort means *one who accompanies,* originally from the Italian word *scorta,* meaning *a guide.* I think that Jade might be a special kind of escort (close your ears, children) also known as a . . . well, you get the idea.

Savvy means *intelligent and insightful.* You learned this word as a synonym for *astute* from an *Austin Powers* excerpt (Group 44). Synonyms: canny, incisive, judicious, keen, perspicacious, sagacious, sage, shrewd, wise. Antonym: obtuse.

Group 47

Here are two excerpts from a movie. See if you can name the movie, describe the scenes, and define the boldface vocabulary words. Check your answers on the following page.

M: No, she's working late tonight. She's trying to **accrue** some extra time off for when . . . you know . . .

J: Behold, good sir! The very first photo of your future child.

M: You're kidding!

J: I think it kind of looks like my friend, Paulie.

M: Oh, is he bald and **amorphous**?

J: No, he's the dad.

———————————

M: Here's to **dovetailing** interests.

J: So, have you and Vanessa thought of a name for the baby yet?

M: Well, sort of. Vanessa likes *Madison* for a girl.

J: *Madison?* Isn't that kind of . . .

M: God, **pretentious** much? I guess everyone should have a mysterious name like . . .

Movie: _____

Scenes: _____

_____

Accrue might mean _____

Amorphous might mean _____

Dovetailing might mean _____

Pretentious might mean _____

Hint: "Like the city in Alaska?"

Solutions

Let's see how you did. Check your answers and write the exact defini-tions. To help you memorize the vocabulary words, reread the movie excerpts or even act out the scenes with a friend.

Movie: *Juno,* Fox Searchlight Pictures, 2007

Scene: Juno (Ellen Page) is a teenager who gets pregnant and is giv-ing her baby up for adoption to Vanessa (Jennifer Garner) and Mark (Jason Bateman). In this scene, Juno is at Vanessa and Mark's house to show them the ultrasound photo. Vanessa isn't home, so Juno winds up hanging out with Mark.

Accrue means *accumulate* or *amass.*

Amorphous means *without a clear form or shape.* Synonyms: nebulous, vague. Paulie (Michael Cera) is not, in fact, amorphous, but he may be virile—in the script, when Juno tells her parents that she's pregnant, her dad says, "Paulie Bleeker? I didn't know he had it in him," to which her stepmom adds, "He just doesn't look . . . well . . . virile." *Virile* means *manly, strong, and energetic* or *with a strong sex drive.* Fortunately for Paulie, this line was left on the editing-room floor.

Dovetailing means *fitting together easily* and is actually a woodworking term for a joint made with pieces of wood that **fit closely together.**

Pretentious means *snobby, showy,* or *conceited, especially in an attempt to impress.* Mark says that Juno is pretentious for judging the name "Madison." Synonyms: affected, ostentatious, pompous.

Group 48

Here's an excerpt from a movie. See if you can name the movie, describe the scene, and define the boldface vocabulary words. Check your answers on the following page.

(Dale enters Saul's apartment.)

SAUL: I didn't buzz you in. How the monkey did you get in here? . . .

DALE: I'm sorry about that. I don't know your **protocol** yet.

SAUL: Ahh, stuff your sorries in a sack, Bro, it's not your fault . . .

DALE: Wow, you've got two TVs and radio. That's pretty rad.

SAUL: Nice home entertainment.

DALE: I'm very entertained. Oh, wow, you've got a cute picture, too.

SAUL: Oh, yeah, me and my Bubbie. Hey, let me ask you something.

DALE: Yeah?

SAUL: Do you think you could pull the plug on someone if you needed to? Like **euthanasia?**

Movie: _____

Scene: _____

_____

Protocol might mean _____

_____

Euthanasia might mean _____

_____

Hint: "I'm more chill than you . . . Look what I'm wearing. Kimono, dog. What are you wearing?"

Solutions

Let's see how you did. Check your answers and write the exact definitions. To help you memorize the vocabulary words, reread the movie excerpt or even act out the scene with a friend.

Movie: *Pineapple Express,* Columbia Pictures, 2008

Scene: This is the first time in the movie that Dale (Seth Rogen) goes to Saul's (James Franco) apartment, and it's when the audience first meets Saul. He's watching *227* on TV and having a great ol' time, *guffawing* (laughing loudly) and eating strawberries dipped in chocolate.

Inside Scoop: James Franco came up with the idea of his character (Saul) having a *Bubbie* (Yiddish for *grandma*). He thought it would be funny for his drug-dealing character to have a Bubbie. I believe he is correct. With *Pineapple Express,* Seth Rogen and the gang were trying to make a funny action movie, and they definitely succeeded. You can see references to lots of famous action films. The hilarious buzzer scene in which Saul and Dale count to three before Saul hits the buzzer is based on a famous scene in *Lethal Weapon 2* between Mel Gibson and Danny Glover. Some of the music in the movie resembles the famous theme song "Axel F," a.k.a. the "Crazy Frog Song," from the *Beverly Hills Cop* movies, and the two thugs that work for Ted (Gary Cole) *parody* (imitate in a funny way) the *Pulp Fiction* bad asses John Travolta and Samuel L. Jackson.

Protocol means *rules for behavior. Star Wars'* C-3PO is a **protocol** *droid* (robot), meaning he helps his owner with the **rules of behavior** when interacting with other cultures. Synonyms: conventions, decorum, etiquette, proprieties, punctilio.

Euthanasia refers to *the practice of painlessly killing a suffering or terminal (dying) patient.* Synonym: quietus.

Group 49

Here are two excerpts from a movie. See if you can name the movie, describe the scenes, and define the boldface vocabulary words. Check your answers on the following page.

REESE BOBBY: (*speaking to his son's class on career day*) Your teacher wants you to go slow, and she's wrong, 'cause it's the fastest who get paid, and it's the fastest who get . . . (*Children in the class cheer.*)

REESE BOBBY: (*being thrown out of the building by security guards*) You people are in the wrong on this one. *So* in the wrong. This is **egregious,** you hear me! Egregious!

———————

SUSAN: Ricky Bobby is not a thinker. Ricky Bobby is a driver . . . And that's what you need to do . . . You need to drive. You need speed. You need to go out there, and you need to rev your engine. You need to fire it up, and you need to grab a hold of that line between speed and **chaos,** and you need to wrestle it to the ground like a demon cobra! And then, when the fear rises up in your belly, you use it . . . And you ride it. You ride it like a skeleton horse through the gates of hell and then you win, Ricky. You *win!* And you don't win for anybody else. You win for you!

Movie: _____

Scenes: _____

_____

_____

Egregious might mean _____

_____

Chaos might mean _____

_____

Hint: (*spoken in a French accent*) "I will let you go, Ricky. But first, I want you to say . . . 'I love crepes.'"

Solutions

Let's see how you did. Check your answers and write the exact definitions. To help you memorize the vocabulary words, reread the movie excerpts or even act out the scenes with a friend.

Movie: *Talladega Nights: The Ballad of Ricky Bobby,* Columbia Pictures, 2006

Scene: In the first excerpt, Reese Bobby (Gary Cole), Ricky's dad, is speaking to Ricky Bobby's class on career day and gets thrown out of the school. In the second excerpt, Ricky Bobby (Will Ferrell) is feeling down and out and bumps into Susan (Amy Adams), who had been his personal assistant. She delivers this inspirational speech and then proceeds to climb onto the table, as Ricky Bobby comments, like the girl in the White Snake video.

Egregious means *shockingly bad*. Synonyms: abhorrent, abominable, appalling, atrocious, dire, grievous, heinous, intolerable.

Chaos means *disorder*. Synonyms: anarchy, bedlam, mayhem, pandemonium, turmoil. I love this quote; *Talladega Nights* might seem like a hilarious yet *nugatory* (meaningless) movie, but there are important messages here. When Ricky Bobby initially dominates stock car racing (NASCAR), he does so for others; he wins to satisfy his wife and to impress his father. But after facing his fears, he drives simply because he likes driving rather than to please someone else. At the end of the movie, he says, "I just went out there and drove and knew that no matter what happened my boys, my momma, and my lady would love me."

Group 50

Here's an excerpt from a movie. See if you can name the movie, describe the scene, and define the boldface vocabulary word. Check your answers on the following page.

DILIOS: The god-king has betrayed a fatal flaw: **Hubris.** Easy to taunt, easy to trick. Before wounds and weariness have taken their toll, the mad king throws the best he has at us. Xerxes has taken the bait.

Movie: _____

Scene: _____

_____

Hubris might mean _____

_____

Hint: "This is Sparta!"

Solutions

Let's see how you did. Check your answers and write the exact definition. To help you memorize the vocabulary word, reread the movie excerpt or even act out the scene with a friend.

Movie: *300,* Warner Bros. Pictures, 2007

Scene: Persian King Xerxes (Rodrigo Santoro) offers Sparta's King Leonidas (Gerard Butler) wealth and power in exchange for his surrender. Leonidas refuses, so Xerxes sends his elite guard, the Immortals, to fight the 300 (the number of soldiers making up Leonidas' personal guard). But King Leonidas and the 300 are ready for them and pleased to face the elite troops early in the battle while the 300 are still strong.

Inside Scoop: This movie is a fictional retelling of the famous Battle of Thermopylae. King Leonidas refers to the battleground as the "hot gates." This is a direct translation of the ancient Greek name, *Thermopylae. Thermo-* means *heat,* as in *thermostat* (a device that regulates temperature), and *-pylae* refers to *gates.*

Hubris means *pride.* Leonidas taunted and offended the **proud** King Xerxes into making a *rash* (reckless) move: Sending in his best troops while the 300 could still resist them. Synonyms: arrogance, conceit, egotism, haughtiness, hauteur, pomposity, superciliousness. Antonym: humility.

Quiz 5

I. Let's review some of the words that you've seen in Groups 41–50. Match each of the following words to the correct definition or synonym on the right. If you need help, refer back to the movie excerpts and definitions. Then check the solutions on page 233.

1. Pinnacle	A. Corrupt
2. Decadence	B. Impuissant
3. Sycophantic	C. Inane
4. Visage	D. Pedestrian
5. Venal	E. Obsequious
6. Vagaries	F. Hedonism
7. Feeble	G. Sagacious
8. Artificial	H. Abhorrent
9. Insipid	I. Ostentatious
10. Astute	J. Fluctuations
11. Wily	K. Apogee
12. Compensate	L. Proprieties
13. Brevity	M. Spurious
14. Fatuous	N. Mayhem
15. Amorphous	O. Face
16. Pretentious	P. Superciliousness
17. Protocol	Q. Nebulous
18. Egregious	R. Machinating
19. Chaos	S. Briefness
20. Hubris	T. Remunerate

II. Let's review several of the word parts that you've seen in Groups 41–50. Match each of the following word parts to the correct definition or synonym on the right. Then check the solutions on page 233.

21. Vagari (as in *vagrant*)	A. With
22. Con- (as in *construct*)	B. Wander

Quiz 5 (continued)

III. Match each group of synonyms to its general meaning. Then check the solutions on page 233.

23. Obsequious
    Oleaginous
    Servile
    Sycophantic
    Toady

A. Shockingly bad

24. Fatuous
    Inane
    Vacuous
    Vapid

B. Pride

25. Astute
    Canny
    Perspicacious
    Sagacious
    Savvy

C. Foolish

26. Abhorrent
    Abominable
    Atrocious
    Dire
    Egregious
    Heinous

D. Overly submissive

27. Conceit
    Egotism
    Haughtiness
    Hubris
    Pomposity
    Superciliousness

E. Shrewd

Here's an excerpt from a movie. See if you can name the movie, describe the scene, and define the boldface vocabulary words. Check your answers on the following page.

VESPER LYND: Ten million was wired to your account in Montenegro, with the **contingency** for five more if I deem it a **prudent** investment. I suppose you've given some thought to the notion that if you lose, our government will have directly financed **terrorism.**

Movie: _____

Scene: _____

_____

Contingency might mean _____

_____

Prudent might mean _____

_____

Terrorism might mean _____

_____

Hint: "Vodka martini. Shaken, not stirred."

Solutions

Let's see how you did. Check your answers and write the exact definitions. To help you memorize the vocabulary words, reread the movie excerpt or even act out the scene with a friend.

Movie: *Casino Royale,* MGM, 2006

Scene: James Bond (Daniel Craig) has just met Vesper Lynd (Eva Green) on the train heading toward Montenegro. She is his contact from the British Treasury and is responsible for providing his $10 million "buy-in" for the Casino Royale poker tournament. After she introduces herself, Bond comments on her name, "*Vesper* . . . I do hope you gave your parents hell for that." *Vesper* means *evening prayer.* Later, Bond invents a mixed drink while playing poker and tells her "You know, I think I'll call that a *Vesper* . . . because once you've tasted it, it's all you want to drink." After he delivers this dashing line, even he can't hold back and comments, "That was quite a good line." Bond's a ladies' man, that's for sure. He might even give Captain Kirk some competition. It would seem, though, that *Family Guy*'s Peter Griffin could teach both of them a thing or two.

Contingency means *possibility* and is often used in the phrase *contingency plan,* which refers to *a plan to deal with a **possible** future event,* such as when Jack of *30 Rock* asks, "What is your contingency plan for a crap storm of this magnitude?" *Magnitude* means *size.* ("Jack Meets Dennis," NBC, 2006) Synonym: eventuality.

Prudent means *sensible, especially with regard to future outcomes.* Synonyms: astute, judicious, sagacious, shrewd. Antonym: myopic (focused on the short term, rather than the future; nearsighted).

Terrorism means *using intimidation, and usually violence, to achieve political goals.* Vesper means that if Bond loses, his buy-in money will wind up in the hands of *terrorists* (people that use terrorism).

Group 52

Here's an excerpt from a movie. See if you can name the movie, describe the scene, and define the boldface vocabulary words. Check your answers on the following page.

S.S.: Don't lie to me! Gillyweed may be **innocuous,** but Boomslang skin? Lacewing flies? You and your little friends are brewing **Polyjuice** Potion, and believe me, I'm going to find out why!

Movie: _____

Scene: _____

_____

Innocuous might mean _____

_____

Polyjuice might mean _____

_____

Hint: "It's a **pensieve,** very useful, if . . . like me, you find your mind a wee bit stretched. It allows me to see once more, things I've already seen. You see, Harry, I've searched and searched for something, some small detail. Something I might have overlooked, something that would explain why these terrible things have happened."

Solutions

Let's see how you did. Check your answers and write the exact definitions. To help you memorize the vocabulary words, reread the movie excerpt or even act out the scene with a friend.

Movie: *Harry Potter and the Goblet of Fire,* Warner Bros., 2005

Scene: OK, "Polyjuice Potion" was a giveaway for this one, but did you remember in which Harry Potter movie Professor Snape (Alan Rickman) accused Harry (Daniel Radcliffe) of stealing it? Surprisingly, in this case it really wasn't Harry's trio that stole it. Barty Crouch, Jr. (David Tennant, of *Dr. Who*) stole the Polyjuice ingredients so that he could impersonate Mad-Eye Moody (Brendan Gleeson).

Vocabulary in the Hint: A *pensieve* is an object used in the *Harry Potter* series to visually review memories. *Pensieve* sounds a lot like *pensive,* which means *thinking deeply,* just like Dumbledore **thinks deeply** as he watches his **thoughts** over and over again in the pensieve, looking for some small detail that he might have overlooked.

Innocuous means *harmless*. *In-* means *not* and *nocuous* is actually a super high-level word for *harmful,* so *innocuous* means *not harmful—harmless.* Synonym: benign.

Polyjuice is an appropriate name for this potion since *poly-* means *many*. The potion turns the user into someone else for a limited time—giving him or her **more than one** physical appearance. *Poly-* also helps you remember words like *polyglot* (a person who speaks **many** languages) and *polyvalent* (having **many** forms or values).

Group 53

Here's an excerpt from a movie. See if you can name the movie, describe the scene, and define the boldface vocabulary words. Check your answers on the following page.

MARTY DIBERGI: This **pretentious, ponderous** collection of religious rock **psalms** is enough to prompt the question, "What day did the Lord create Spinal Tap, and couldn't he have rested on that day, too?"

Movie: _____

Scene: _____

_____

Pretentious might mean _____

_____

Ponderous might mean _____

_____

Psalms might mean _____

_____

Hint: Part of the name of the movie is in the quote.

Solutions

Let's see how you did. Check your answers and write the exact definitions. To help you memorize the vocabulary words, reread the movie excerpt or even act out the scene with a friend.

Movie: *This Is Spinal Tap,* Embassy Pictures, 1984

Scene: Marty (Rob Reiner) is reading a review of Spinal Tap's latest album. If you have not seen this movie, you should. It's a hilarious mock *rockumentary* (a documentary about rock music) of the fictitious band Spinal Tap. You've probably heard a few of their songs, perhaps "Big Bottom" or "Stonehenge," and you may have heard famous quotes such as, "These go to eleven," or "It's such a fine line between stupid and clever." That last quote, like the whole movie, is either quite insightful or completely moronic.

Pretentious means *snobby, showy,* or *conceited, especially in an attempt to impress.* Quiz: In what movie/group did you learn this word? Hint: Orange Tic Tacs. Answer: *Juno* (Group 47). In that movie, Mark (Jason Bateman) said that Juno (Ellen Page) is **pretentious** for judging the name "Madison." Synonyms: affected, ostentatious, pompous.

Ponderous means *heavy and awkward* or *dull.* This looks like the word *ponder* (think deeply). If one **pondered** before every action, life might get pretty **slow moving** and **dull.** Synonyms: laborious, lifeless, maladroit, monotonous, pedestrian, plodding, stilted, stodgy, tedious. The opposite of *ponderous* is *animated.*

Psalms means *sacred songs or hymns.* The reviewer referred to Spinal Tap's music as *rock psalms* to show that the songs are too dramatic for rock songs.

Here's the translation of the excerpt:

"This **snobby, conceited, awkward, and dull** collection of religious rock **hymns** is enough to . . . " The reviewer is definitely not a fan of Spinal Tap.

Group 54

Here's an excerpt from a movie. See if you can name the movie, describe the scene, and define the boldface vocabulary words. Check your answers on the following page.

ELWOOD: You may go if you wish. But remember this: walk away now and you walk away from your crafts, your skills, your **vocations;** leaving the next generation with nothing but recycled, digitally sampled techno grooves; **quasi**-synth rhythms; **pseudo**-songs of violence-laden gangsta-rap; acid pop; and **simpering, saccharine,** soulless slush. Depart now and you forever separate yourselves from the **vital** American legacies of Robert Johnson, Muddy Waters, Willie Dixon, Jimmy Reed, Memphis Slim, Blind Boy Fuller, Louie Jordan, Little Walter, Big Walter, Sonny Boy Williamson I and II, Otis Redding, Jackie Wilson, Elvis Presley, Lieber and Stoller, and Robert K. Weiss.

Movie: _____

Scene: _____

_____

Vocations might mean _____

Quasi might mean _____

Pseudo might mean _____

Simpering might mean _____

Saccharine might mean _____

Vital might mean _____

Hint: This movie features musical guests Blues Traveler, Wilson Pickett, Aretha Franklin, James Brown, Paul Shaffer, Erykah Badu, B. B. King, Eric Clapton, Clarence Clemons, Bo Diddley, Lou Rawls, Travis Tritt, Jimmie Vaughan, Steve Winwood, and many, many more.

Solutions

Let's see how you did. Check your answers and write the exact definitions. To help you memorize the vocabulary words, reread the movie excerpt or even act out the scene with a friend.

Movie: *Blues Brothers 2000,* Universal Pictures, 1998

Scene: This is Elwood Blues (Dan Aykroyd) motivational speech to keep the Blues Brothers band together after many trials and *tribulations* (hardships).

Vocations means *occupations that people are well suited for or even "called" to do.* Synonym: métiers.

Quasi means *supposed* or *partial.*

Pseudo is similar to *quasi* and means *fake. Pseudo* reminds me of the word *artificial,* which you learned in Group 42, *The Matrix: Revolutions.* Synonyms for *pseudo:* bogus, contrived, ersatz, mock, phony, sham, spurious.

Simpering means *insincerely and flirtatiously cute and shy.*

Saccharine looks like the word for the artificial **sweetener** saccharin and is a fancy word for *overly **sweet** or sentimental.* Synonyms: cloying, mawkish, treacly.

Vital means *essential.*

Here's the translation of the excerpt using the definitions on this page:

> ELWOOD: You may go if you wish. But remember this: walk away now and you walk away from your crafts, your skills, your **occupations;** leaving the next generation with nothing but recycled, digitally sampled techno grooves, **partial**-synth rhythms, **fake**-songs of violence-laden gangsta rap; acid pop; and **insincerely cute and shy, overly sentimental,** soulless slush. Depart now and you forever separate yourselves from the **essential** American legacies of . . .

Group 55

Here are two excerpts from a movie. See if you can name the movie, describe the scenes, and define the boldface vocabulary words. Check your answers on the following page.

DEAN WORMER: Then as of this moment, they're on *double secret probation!*

GREG: Double secret probation, Sir?

DEAN WORMER: There is a little-known **codicil** in the Faber College constitution which gives the Dean unlimited power to preserve order in time of campus emergency. Find me a way to **revoke** Delta's charter.

OTTER: Bluto's right. Psychotic, but absolutely right. We gotta take these bastards. Now we could fight 'em with **conventional** weapons that could take years and cost millions of lives. No, in this case, I think we have to go all out. I think that this situation absolutely requires a really **futile** and stupid gesture be done on somebody's part.

BLUTO: And we're just the guys to do it.

Movie: _____

Scenes: _____

_____

Probation might mean _____

Codicil might mean _____

Revoke might mean _____

Conventional might mean _____

Futile might mean _____

Hint: "Toga! Toga!"

Solutions

Let's see how you did. Check your answers and write the exact definitions. To help you memorize the vocabulary words, reread the movie excerpts or even act out the scenes with a friend.

Movie: *National Lampoon's Animal House,* Universal Pictures, 1978

Scenes: The Dean (John Vernon) of Faber College hates the Delta House fraternity (a.k.a. Animal House) and wants them kicked out of school. He stoops pretty low to do it. In the second quote, the fraternity plans their revenge. This is a classic movie and a must-see for any college hopeful. *Animal House* is the original *Old School*.

Probation means *period of testing or observation.*

Codicil means *addition,* like an amendment to the U.S. Constitution. Synonyms: amendment, appendix, corollary.

Revoke means *cancel.* Synonym: countermand.

Conventional means *traditional* or *ordinary.* "*Conventional weapons*" means *guns, mines, and bombs, but **not** nuclear, chemical, or biological weapons.*

Futile means *pointless.* Synonyms: absurd, fatuous, inane, nugatory, vacuous, vain, vapid. You learned *fatuous* from *The Big Lebowski* in Group 45.

Group 56

Here's an excerpt from a movie. See if you can name the movie, describe the scene, and define the boldface vocabulary words. Check your answers on the following page.

TARKIN: The **Imperial** Senate will no longer be of any concern to us. I have just received word that the Emperor has dissolved the council permanently. The last remnants of the Old **Republic** have been swept away.

TAGGE: But that's impossible. How will the Emperor maintain control without the **bureaucracy?** . . . And what of the Rebellion? If the Rebels have obtained a complete technical readout of this station, it is possible, however unlikely, that they might find a weakness and **exploit** it.

VADER: The plans you refer to will soon be back in our hands . . .

MOTTI: Don't try to frighten us with your sorcerer's ways . . . Your sad devotion to that ancient religion has not helped you **conjure** up the stolen data tapes, or given you **clairvoyance** enough to find the Rebels' hidden fortress . . .

Movie: _____

Scene: _____

Imperial might mean _____

Republic might mean _____

Bureaucracy might mean _____

Exploit might mean _____

Conjure might mean _____

Clairvoyance might mean _____

Hint: "**Hokey** religions and ancient weapons are no match for a good blaster at your side, kid."

Solutions

Let's see how you did. Check your answers and write the exact definitions. To help you memorize the vocabulary words, reread the movie excerpt or even act out the scene with a friend.

Movie: *Star Wars Episode IV: A New Hope,* 20th Century Fox, 1977

Scene: This is the famous scene in which Admiral Motti disrespects the Force to Darth Vader, who then raises his arm and pinches the air, using the Force to choke Motti from a distance. In the hint, Han Solo (Harrison Ford) also doubts the power of the Force, but thankfully Luke (Mark Hamill) and Obi-Wan (Alec Guinness) are more forgiving of his lack of faith.

Vocabulary in the Hint: *Hokey* means *corny, overused,* or *overly sentimental.* Standardized tests love the related words *banal* (overused and boring), *cliché, hackneyed, platitudinous,* and *trite,* which mean *overused.* In this quote, Han Solo is saying that Obi-Wan's religion (the Force) is **overly sentimental** and that light sabers are outdated. They'll soon prove him wrong; in fact, one thing that made *Star Wars* so original back in 1977 was its portrayal of humanity as ultimately more powerful than technology.

Imperial means *relating to an empire.* It can also mean *bossy* or *domineering,* which makes sense since an empire is usually pretty domineering. Synonym: imperious. Know that word? Think *Harry Potter.* The **Imperius** Curse, one of the three Unforgivable Curses, gives you complete **control** over another person, a pretty **domineering** thing to do. J. K. Rowling, like George Lucas, is looking out for your test scores!

Republic means *a group ruled by its people or by an elected ruler, rather than an all-powerful king, queen, or emperor.*

Bureaucracy means *the officials and administrative procedures of a government.*

Exploit means *use to one's advantage.* Synonym: capitalize on.

Conjure means *materialize* or *summon.*

Clairvoyance means *psychic powers,* often used to predict the future. Synonym: prescience.

Group 57

Here's an excerpt from a movie. See if you can name the movie, describe the scene, and define the boldface vocabulary words. Check your answers on the following page.

U.S. Marshal Larkin: We got you a seat right next to him, and he's known to be somewhat **garrulous** in the company of thieves.

Agent Malloy: Garrulous. What the f#*% is garrulous?

U.S. Marshal Larkin: That would be **loquacious, verbose, effusive,** how about "chatty"?

Agent Malloy: What's with Dictionary Boy?

U.S. Marshal Larkin: Thesaurus Boy, I think, is more appropriate.

Movie: _____

Scene: _____

_____

Garrulous might mean _____

_____

Loquacious might mean _____

_____

Verbose might mean _____

_____

Effusive might mean _____

_____

Hint: This 1997 movie starred Nicolas Cage kicking butt aboard an airplane of convicts.

Solutions

Let's see how you did. Check your answers and write the exact definitions. To help you memorize the vocabulary words, reread the movie excerpt or even act out the scene with a friend.

Movie: *Con Air,* Touchstone Pictures, 1997

Scene: U.S. Marshal Vince Larkin (John Cusack) is speaking with DEA Agent Malloy (Colm Meaney). They are placing an undercover agent on board an airplane that is transporting prisoners. The agent is assigned to get information from a convict with ties to organized crime. Larkin says that the convict is chatty with other convicts and should be easy to get information from. They did not plan on the convicts taking over the plane, *but* those convicts did not plan on elite ex-Army Ranger Cameron Poe (Nicolas Cage) being on board!

Garrulous means *talkative.* Synonyms: effusive, expansive, loquacious, prolix, verbose, voluble. Antonyms: reticent, taciturn.

Loquacious means *talkative.* Synonyms: effusive, expansive, garrulous, prolix, verbose, voluble. Antonyms: reticent, taciturn. In *Harry Potter and the Goblet of Fire,* Hermione comments that Krum is not very **loquacious** and just likes to watch her study. It's true; Krum is not very chatty, though he's a mighty fine Seeker.

Verbose means *wordy.* Synonyms: effusive, expansive, garrulous, loquacious, prolix, voluble. Antonyms: concise, laconic, reticent, succinct, taciturn.

Effusive means *gushing, unrestrained speaking or writing.* Synonyms: expansive, garrulous, loquacious, prolix, verbose, voluble. Antonyms: restrained, reticent, taciturn.

Group 58

Here are two excerpts from a movie. See if you can name the movie, describe the scenes, and define the boldface vocabulary words. Check your answers on the following page.

ADRIAN VEIDT: Well, it was **unprecedented.** I wanted . . . *needed* to match his accomplishments, and so I resolved to apply **antiquity's** teaching to our world, *today*. And so began my path to conquest. Conquest not of men, but of the evils that **beset** them.

———————

ADRIAN VEIDT: You understand, don't you?

JON OSTERMAN: Without **condoning** . . . or **condemning.** I understand.

Movie: _____

Scenes: _____

_____

Unprecedented might mean _____

Antiquity might mean _____

Beset might mean _____

Condoning might mean _____

Condemning might mean _____

Hint: A yellow smiley face with a drop of blood on it.

Solutions

Let's see how you did. Check your answers and write the exact definitions. To help you memorize the vocabulary words, reread the movie excerpts or even act out the scenes with a friend.

Movie: *Watchmen,* Warner Bros., 2009

Scenes: This is a superhero film set during the Cold War of the 1980s that is based on the *Watchmen* comic books by Alan Moore and Dave Gibbons. In the first scene, Veidt/Ozymandias (Matthew Goode) is speaking with heads of industry just before an anonymous gunman attempts to assassinate him. In the second scene, he is explaining to Jon/Dr. Manhattan (Billy Crudup), Dan/Nite Owl (Patrick Wilson), Rorschach (Jackie Earle Haley), and Laurie/Silk Spectre (Malin Åkerman) why he did what he did.

Unprecedented means *totally new, never seen before. Un-* means *not* or *lack of,* and *precedent* means *earlier example,* so *unprecedented* means *lack of earlier example—totally new, never seen before.*

Antiquity means *the past,* so when Veidt says "antiquity's teaching" he means "lessons of the past."

Beset means *trouble* or *afflict.* Synonyms: assail, bedevil, beleaguer, besiege, harass, oppress, plague, torment.

Condoning means *reluctantly approving or allowing.* Synonym: sanctioning.

Condemning means *strongly disapproving.* Synonyms: censuring, denouncing, rebuking, reproaching, reproving. Jon (Dr. Manhattan) is less and less invested in humans and the planet Earth so it would make sense that he neither **condones** (approves) nor **condemns** (disapproves), he just sees and acknowledges. You could say that he's *apathetic, dispassionate, indifferent,* or *insouciant* (all meaning *uninterested,* as you learned in Group 8) and that's why he decides to leave for another galaxy.

Group 59

Here's an excerpt from a movie. See if you can name the movie, describe the scene, and define the boldface vocabulary words. Check your answers on the following page.

NARRATOR: It began with the forging of the Great Rings. Three were given to the Elves; **immortal,** wisest, and **fairest** of all beings. Seven to the Dwarf Lords, great miners and craftsmen of the mountain halls. And nine, nine rings were gifted to the race of Men, who above all else desire power . . . In the fires of Mount Doom, the Dark Lord Sauron forged in secret a master ring to control all others. And into this ring he poured all his cruelty, his **malice,** and his will to dominate all life. One ring to rule them all . . . And some things that should not have been forgotten were lost. History became legend. Legend became myth. And for two and a half thousand years, the ring passed out of all knowledge. Until, when chance came, the ring **ensnared** another bearer . . .

Movie: _____

Scene: _____

Immortal might mean _____

_____

Fairest might mean _____

_____

Malice might mean _____

_____

Ensnared might mean _____

_____

Hint: "My precious . . . "

Solutions

Let's see how you did. Check your answers and write the exact definitions. To help you memorize the vocabulary words, reread the movie excerpt or even act out the scene with a friend.

Movie: *The Lord of the Rings: The Fellowship of the Ring,* New Line Cinema, 2001

Scene: Jim and the guys are at a party at Stifler's house at the beginning of the movie. No, just kidding. This is the narration by Galadriel, Queen of Lothlórien (Cate Blanchett), at the beginning of the movie. Even the movie's title has vocab in it. *Fellowship* means *association of people (or elves, dwarves, and hobbits) with a shared interest.* Synonyms: brotherhood, fraternity, guild, sisterhood, sodality, sorority. *Fellowship* can also simply mean *friendship.*

Immortal means *never dying.* Synonyms: ceaseless, eternal, everlasting, immutable, imperishable, inextinguishable, intransient, perpetual. Antonyms: ephemeral, evanescent, fleeting, mortal, transient.

Fairest in this case means *beautiful,* as in "Mirror, mirror on the wall, who's the **fairest** of them all?" Synonyms: pulchritudinous, winsome.

Malice means *ill will* and is described in the excerpt by Sauron's "cruelty" and "will to dominate all life." That's the same way that standardized tests work; in reading test questions, the tested word is always described or even defined nearby. Galadriel does it here, Bruce Wayne did it in *Batman Begins* when he said, "You sycophantic suck-ups" (Group 41), and the SAT does it, too. Synonyms: animus, enmity, maleficence, malevolence, malignity, rancor, spite, vengefulness, vindictiveness. The opposite of *malice* is *benevolence* (good will).

Ensnared means *caught* or *trapped.* Synonyms: embroiled, enmeshed, entangled. Do you remember whom the ring ensnared? "My precious . . . "

Group 60

Here's an excerpt from a movie. See if you can name the movie, describe the scene, and define the boldface vocabulary words. Check your answers on the following page.

Evan: It's not just making them smaller. They completely reshape them. They make them more **supple** and **symmetrical.**

Seth: I gotta catch a glimpse of these warlocks. Let's make a move.

Movie: _____

Scene: _____

_____

Supple might mean _____

_____

Symmetrical might mean _____

_____

Hint: "I am McLovin'!"

Solutions

Let's see how you did. Check your answers and write the exact definitions. To help you memorize the vocabulary words, reread the movie excerpt or even act out the scene with a friend.

Movie: *Superbad,* Columbia Pictures, 2007

Scene: Do you remember what Evan (Michael Cera) and Seth (Jonah Hill) are talking about? If not, you'll have to rewatch *Superbad.* I can't say too much more or else my editors will realize what the guys are talking about and cut this excerpt from the book.

Inside Scoop: Because Fogell (Christopher Mintz-Plasse) was a minor during the filming of *Superbad*, his mother had to be on set during the filming of his "sex scene" with Nicola.

Supple means *soft, flexible, and graceful.* Synonyms: agile, limber, lissome, lithe, malleable, nimble, pliable, pliant, willowy. Antonym: rigid.

Symmetrical means *evenly proportioned. Sym-* means *together,* as in *symbiotic* (*bio-* refers to *life,* so *symbiotic* means "life together"—*a mutually beneficial relationship*), and *metrical* refers to *measurement,* so *symmetrical* means *measurement together—evenly proportioned.*

Quiz 6

I. Let's review some of the words that you've seen in Groups 51–60. Match each of the following words to the correct definition or synonym on the right. If you need help, refer back to the movie excerpts and definitions. Then check the solutions on page 234.

1. Contingency	A. Judicious
2. Prudent	B. Occupation
3. Innocuous	C. Corollary
4. Ponderous	D. Trite
5. Vocation	E. Eventuality
6. Saccharine	F. Verbose
7. Codicil	G. Laborious
8. Futile	H. Censure
9. Hokey	I. Lithe
10. Imperious	J. Enmity
11. Clairvoyance	K. Cloying
12. Garrulous	L. Benign
13. Condemn	M. Prescience
14. Malice	N. Nugatory
15. Supple	O. Domineering

II. Let's review several of the word parts that you've seen in Groups 51–60. Match each of the following word parts to the correct definition or synonym on the right. Then check the solutions on page 234.

16. In- (as in *innocuous*)	A. Together
17. Poly- (as in *polyglot*)	B. Not
18. Bio- (as in *symbiotic*)	C. Across
19. Sym- (as in *symmetrical*)	D. One
Review from earlier groups:	E. Many
20. Trans- (as in *transcription*)	F. Life
21. Mono- (as in *monarchy*)	

III. Match each group of synonyms to its general meaning. Then check the solutions on page 234.

22. Laborious Maladroit Pedestrian Ponderous Stilted	A. Overly sentimental	
23. Bogus Contrived Ersatz Pseudo Spurious	B. Pointless	
24. Cloying Mawkish Saccharine Treacly	C. Heavy and awkward or dull	
25. Fatuous Futile Inane Nugatory Vacuous Vain Vapid	D. Talkative	
26. Banal Cliché Hackneyed Hokey Platitudinous Trite	E. Corny, overused	
27. Effusive Garrulous Loquacious Prolix Verbose Voluble	F. Fake	

Group 61

Here's an excerpt from a movie. See if you can name the movie, describe the scene, and define the boldface vocabulary word. Check your answers on the following page.

JOHN BECKWITH: (*discussing Chaz*) He lived with his mother 'til he was forty! She tried to poison his oatmeal!

JEREMY GREY: Erroneous! **Erroneous!** Erroneous on both counts!

Movie: _____

Scene: _____

_____

Erroneous might mean _____

_____

Hint: "They're not who they say they are, Claire. Those aren't even their real names . . . Everything that they've told us is a complete **fabrication.**"

Solutions

Let's see how you did. Check your answers and write the exact definition. To help you memorize the vocabulary word, reread the movie excerpt or even act out the scene with a friend.

Movie: *Wedding Crashers,* New Line Cinema, 2005

Scene: Jeremy (Vince Vaughn) is trying to convince John (Owen Wilson) to go to a wedding and he brings up Chaz. We later meet Chaz, played by Will Ferrell. He was Jeremy's mentor, and the one who passed down the sacred rules of Wedding Crashing. I find this movie oddly inspiring. I don't aspire to crash weddings, but I appreciate the friendship between John and Jeremy and the transformation and insight of John's character as he falls in love with Claire (Rachel McAdams) and goes from insensitive, unethical wedding crasher to sensitive, honest romantic.

Inside Scoop: Did you recognize Bradley Cooper (now famous as Phil from *The Hangover*) as Zack, Claire's obnoxious boyfriend?

Vocabulary in the Hint: *Fabrication* means *lie.* Specifically, it means *an invented story or excuse.* Good use of the word, Zack! In John and Jeremy's current **fabrication** they are Uncle Ned's kids working as venture capitalists in New Hampshire. They have also been Lou Epstein and Chuck Schwartz, Sanjay Collins and Chuck Vindaloo, and Seamus O'Toole and Bobby O'Shea. Synonyms: equivocation, prevarication.

Erroneous means *incorrect* and even sounds like the word *error.* In fact, *-ous* means *characterized by,* so *erroneous* means *characterized by errors—incorrect.* Synonyms: fallacious, specious.

Group 62

Here's an excerpt from a movie. See if you can name the movie, describe the scene, and define the boldface vocabulary words. Check your answers on the following page.

DENNIS: Oh king, eh, very nice. And how d'you get that, eh? By **exploiting** the workers! By 'anging on to outdated **imperialist dogma** which **perpetuates** the economic and social differences in our society. If there's ever going to be any progress with the . . .

WOMAN: I didn't know we had a king. I thought we were an **autonomous** collective.

DENNIS: You're fooling yourself. We're living in a **dictatorship.** A self-perpetuating **autocracy** in which the working classes . . .

ARTHUR: Please, please good people. I am in **haste.** Who lives in that castle?

WOMAN: No one lives there.

ARTHUR: Then who is your lord?

WOMAN: We don't have a lord.

ARTHUR: What?

DENNIS: I told you. We're an **anarcho~syndicalist** commune. We take it in turns to act as a sort of executive officer for the week.

Movie: _____

Scene: _____

_____

Hint: "Arthur, King of the Britons, your Knights of the Round Table shall have a task to make them an example in these dark times . . ."

Group 62 (continued)

Exploiting might mean _____

_____

Imperialist might mean _____

_____

Dogma might mean _____

_____

Perpetuates might mean _____

_____

Autonomous might mean _____

_____

Dictatorship might mean _____

_____

Autocracy might mean _____

_____

Haste might mean _____

_____

Anarcho-syndicalist might mean _____

_____

Solutions

Let's see how you did. Check your answers and write the exact definitions. To help you memorize the vocabulary words, reread the movie excerpt or even act out the scene with a friend.

Movie: *Monty Python and the Holy Grail,* Fox, 1975

Scene: King Arthur (Graham Chapman) is traveling around looking for knights to join his quest when he meets Dennis, an old ~~woman~~ man who is only thirty-seven and spouts out some excellent lines. Dennis and his wife were digging filth along the path, but wind up in a heated political argument with Arthur.

Solutions (continued)

Exploiting means *taking advantage of*. Synonym: capitalizing on.

Imperialist means *royal* or *imposing,* like the **Imperial** Stormtroopers in *Star Wars,* the **imperial** palace in China, or the forbidden **Imperius** Curse in the *Harry Potter* books and movies that allows the caster to *impose* his or her will over the target of the spell.

Dogma means *system of beliefs presented as indisputable*. Synonyms: canon, creed, doctrine, precept, tenet.

Perpetuates means *continues*.

Autonomous means *self-governing*. *Auto-* means *self,* as in *autocrat* (a ruler who holds all the power by him- or her**self**). Synonyms: independent, sovereign.

Dictatorship and **autocracy** both mean *government ruled by one individual with complete power*—the one person **dictates** everything.

Haste means *a rush,* as in a *hasty* (rushed) decision or the third-level wizard spell in Dungeons & Dragons that makes a character act more **quickly.**

Anarcho-syndicalist refers to a *system of government self-managed by workers. Anarcho-* refers to *anarchism* (the belief in total individual freedom), and *syndicalist* refers to *an economic system to replace capitalism in which everything is owned by workers' unions.* Can you believe that *anarcho-syndicalist* is a real word? I bet you thought that Monty Python made all this stuff up!

Group 63

Here's an excerpt from a movie. See if you can name the movie, describe the scene, and define the boldface vocabulary words. Check your answers on the following page.

A.D.: Cornelius, I *implore* you to see reason. The evidence that the Dark Lord has returned is **incontrovertible.**

Movie: _____

Scene: _____

_____

Implore might mean _____

_____

Incontrovertible might mean _____

_____

Hint: "The time has come for answers, whether he wants to give them or not. Have you brought the **Veritaserum**?"

Solutions

Let's see how you did. Check your answers and write the exact definitions. To help you memorize the vocabulary words, reread the movie excerpt or even act out the scene with a friend.

Movie: *Harry Potter and the Order of the Phoenix,* Warner Bros., 2007

Scene: Albus Dumbledore (Michael Gambon) said this to Minister of Magic Cornelius Fudge (Robert Hardy) while defending Harry (Daniel Radcliffe) in front of the Wizengamot. Harry is being tried for having used magic to protect Dudley and himself from Dementors at the beginning of the film.

Vocabulary in the Hint: J. K. Rowling loves to use great vocab words to name characters and magical items in the *Harry Potter* universe, and there are a few in the hint. The quote in the hint is from Dolores Umbridge (Imelda Staunton) who takes over Hogwarts School of Witchcraft and Wizardry. She is usually pretty angry and annoyed, and in fact, the word *umbrage* means *anger and annoyance!* Also, *Veritaserum* (**truth** serum) contains the root word *veri-*, meaning *truth.* That can help you remember words like *verity* (a fundamental **truth**), *verify* (confirm the **truth** of), and the word you learned from *American Pie* (Group 1), *verisimilitude* (the appearance of seeming real or **true**)!

Implore means *beg.* Synonyms: beseech, entreat, importune.

Incontrovertible means *unquestionable.* This is a great word to break apart. *In-* means *not,* and *controvert* means *deny,* so *incontrovertible* means *not deniable—unquestionable.* Synonyms: conclusive, indisputable, indubitable, irrefutable, unassailable.

Group 64

Here's an excerpt from a movie. See if you can name the movie, describe the scene, and define the boldface vocabulary word. Check your answers on the following page.

KUMAR PATEL: I fear that I will always be
A lonely number like root three . . .
I wish instead I were a nine
For nine could **thwart** this evil trick,
with just some quick arithmetic.

Movie: _____

Scene: _____

_____

Thwart might mean _____

_____

Hint: This time they're not headed to White Castle.

Solutions

Let's see how you did. Check your answers and write the exact definition. To help you memorize the vocabulary word, reread the movie excerpt or even act out the scene with a friend.

Movie: *Harold & Kumar Escape from Guantanamo Bay,* Warner Bros., 2008

Scene: This is the love poem that Kumar recites to Vanessa when he interrupts her wedding and tries to win her back.

Inside Scoop: In April 2009, Kal Penn, who plays Kumar, accepted a position from President Obama as *liaison* (representative) to Asian-American groups. Officially, he is Associate Director of the White House Office of Public Engagement! I'm not messing with you; this is true. That's why his *House, M.D.* character had to be killed off. But, don't assume his pot-smoking character, Kumar, is now working in the White House. In real life, Kal does not smoke pot or drink alcohol, is a strict vegetarian, attended UCLA and Stanford, and taught Asian-American Studies at the University of Pennsylvania! Interestingly, at UPenn he taught a class called "Contemporary American Teen Films." This book could have been a required text!

Thwart means *prevent* or *block progress of.* Synonyms: forestall, stonewall, stymie.

Group 65

Here are two excerpts from a movie. See if you can name the movie, describe the scenes, and define the boldface vocabulary words. Check your answers on the following page.

PRELUDE: She was a **comely** young woman and not without prospects. Therefore, it was heartbreaking to her mother that she would enter into marriage with William Munny, a known thief and murderer, a man of **notoriously** vicious and **intemperate disposition.**

EPILOGUE: Some years later, Mrs. Ansonia Feathers made the **arduous** journey to Hodgeman County to visit the last resting place of her only daughter. William Munny had long since disappeared with the children . . . some said to San Francisco where it was rumored he **prospered** in dry goods. And there was nothing on the marker to explain to Mrs. Feathers why her only daughter had married a known thief and murderer, a man of notoriously vicious and intemperate disposition.

Movie: _____

Scenes: _____

Comely might mean _____

Notoriously might mean _____

Intemperate might mean _____

Disposition might mean _____

Arduous might mean _____

Prospered might mean _____

Hint: "I've always been lucky when it comes to killin' folks." There's only one actor that can earnestly deliver a line like this, and he won an Academy Award for this film in 1992. His most famous line before this movie was, "Go ahead, make my day."

Solutions

Let's see how you did. Check your answers and write the exact definitions. To help you memorize the vocabulary words, reread the movie excerpts or even act out the scenes with a friend.

Movie: *Unforgiven,* Warner Bros., 1992

Scenes: This was a tough one. Did the hint help? You've probably seen this classic on television late at night. *Unforgiven* is a powerful movie about an ex-gunslinger trying to make good. The first excerpt is the *prelude* (introduction) printed on the screen at the opening of the movie, and the second excerpt is the *epilogue* (conclusion) printed on the screen at the end of the film.

Comely means *attractive.* Synonyms: beauteous, fair, fetching, prepossessing, pulchritudinous. Here's why I'm a vocabulary teacher. While everyone else's dad calls their mom "beautiful," my dad uses the *endearment* (affectionate expression) "pulchy," short for *pulchritudinous!*

Notoriously looks like *notably* and means *well known for bad things,* sort of like *famous,* but *famous for **bad things**.* Why do you think that rapper Christopher George Latore Wallace chose the stage name *The Notorious B.I.G.,* and whom do you think is tougher, Clint's cowboy or rapper Biggie? Either way, Biggie is not quite as intimidating when you call him Christopher. Synonyms: infamously, scandalously.

Intemperate means *lacking self-control.* Remember from *Monty Python and the Holy Grail* (Group 31) that *temperate* means *mild* or *restrained,* and since *in-* means *not, intemperate* means *not restrained—lacking self-control.* Synonyms: immoderate, prodigal, profligate, unrestrained, wanton.

Disposition means *personality* or *character.* Synonyms: constitution, temperament.

Arduous means *difficult and requiring hard work.* Synonyms: Herculean, laborious, onerous, toilsome.

Prospered means *thrived.* Synonyms: blossomed, burgeoned, flourished. Clint Eastwood's character was a pretty tough and *ornery* (bad-tempered) cowboy, so I'm not so sure he'd take kindly to the synonym "blossomed." We'll just keep that one to ourselves, OK?

Group 66

Here's an excerpt from a movie. See if you can name the movie, describe the scene, and define the boldface vocabulary word. Check your answers on the following page.

O.K.: You and the Naboo form a **symbiont** circle. What happens to one of you will affect the other.

Movie: _____

Scene: _____

_____

Symbiont might mean _____

_____

Hint: "I have encountered a **vergence** in the Force."

Solutions

Let's see how you did. Check your answers and write the exact definition. To help you memorize the vocabulary word, reread the movie excerpt or even act out the scene with a friend.

Movie: *Star Wars Episode I: The Phantom Menace,* 20th Century Fox, 1999

Scene: Obi-Wan Kenobi (Ewan McGregor) is explaining to Jar Jar Binks why the Gungans and the Naboo must work together.

Inside Scoop: Frank Oz is the voice and puppeteer for Jedi Master Yoda, and interestingly, he is also the voice and puppeteer for the Muppets' Miss Piggy, Fozzie Bear, and Animal, as well as *Sesame Street* characters Grover, Cookie Monster, and Bert! Amazing! I knew the Force was strong with Cookie Monster!

Vocabulary in the Hint: *Vergence* means *coming together.* It's actually a medical term for when *the pupils of the eyes* ***move together*** *in unison either toward or away from each other,* but George Lucas is using it liberally in *Star Wars*. He probably wanted to use a word that sounds impressive and catches the movie viewers' attention. "A vergence in the Force" means that the midi-chlorians **come together** more than is usual in Anakin—that's how Qui-Gon Jinn (Liam Neeson) and Obi-Wan know Anakin is the Chosen One (who will bring balance to the Force).

Symbiont means *mutually beneficial.* It's a form of the word *symbiotic,* which also means *mutually beneficial.* This is an interesting word to break apart. *Sym-* means *together,* as in *symmetrical* (measured together—evenly proportioned) and *sympathy* (feeling together—compassion), and *bio-* means *life,* so *symbiont* means *life together—mutually beneficial.*

Group 67

Here's an excerpt from a movie. See if you can name the movie, describe the scene, and define the boldface vocabulary words. Check your answers on the following page.

TECH: I have a hit on **echelon** "Blackbriar." I repeat "Blackbriar." Looks like it's coming from a European signal. NSA, please confirm receipt . . .

VOSEN: Who talked to him? How did he find out about Blackbriar?

WILLS: We don't know, we pulled his background and have run a crosscheck on any known **anomalies.** We've come up with nothing. But, I think if we follow Ross, we are going to be able . . .

VOSEN: Right. Ross is easy. We want the source. I want **rendition protocols** and put the **asset** on standby, just in case.

Movie: _____

Scene: _____

Echelon might mean _____

_____

Anomalies might mean _____

_____

Rendition might mean _____

_____

Protocols might mean _____

_____

Asset might mean _____

_____

Hint: "Nicky Parsons has **compromised** a **covert** operation. She is up to her neck in this."

Solutions

Let's see how you did. Check your answers and write the exact definitions. To help you memorize the vocabulary words, reread the movie excerpt or even act out the scene with a friend.

Movie: *The Bourne Ultimatum,* Universal Pictures, 2007

Scene: CIA Deputy Director Vosen (David Strathairn) is alerted that a journalist, Ross (Paddy Considine), used the codeword *Blackbriar* during a phone call. Vosen issues an NSA Priority Level Four Alert to track Ross and find his source.

Vocabulary in the Hint: *Compromised* in this case means *endangered* or *weakened.* Synonym: jeopardized. Of course, *compromised* can also mean *made concessions to arrive at an agreement. Covert* sounds like *covered* and means *hidden* or *secret.* Synonyms: clandestine, furtive, surreptitious. The opposite of *covert* (secret) is *overt* (obvious).

Echelon means *level.* It was a high-**level** hit. Blackbriar is "above top secret," so when the CIA overhears Ross saying such a high-**level** codeword, it triggers a high-level response, an NSA Priority Level Four Alert.

Anomalies means *irregularities.* Synonyms: aberrations, incongruities.

Rendition in this case means *covert extradition* (secretly moving a criminal or criminal suspect from one country to another).

Protocols means *procedures.* So "rendition protocols" means *the procedures to secretly move a criminal or suspected criminal* (Vosen's referring to Matt Damon's character, Jason Bourne) *from one country to another.* Jason Bourne is like Rambo, you just don't want to cross this guy, though Vosen is determined to learn that the hard way.

Asset in this case means *assassin.* Future accounting majors, you're about to have your hero-moment here, because believe it or not this term is actually borrowed from accounting, which is interesting because one doesn't usually link *accountants* with *assassins.* In accounting, *asset* means *resource,* and Vosen's **resource** is an **assassin** to send after Bourne.

Group 68

Here's an excerpt from a movie. See if you can name the movie, describe the scene, and define the boldface vocabulary words. Check your answers on the following page.

THE BOOK: Vogons are one of the most unpleasant races in the galaxy. Not evil, but bad-tempered, **bureaucratic, officious,** and **callous.** They wouldn't even lift a finger to save their own grandmothers from the **ravenous** Bug-Blatter Beast of Traal without orders signed in triplicate, sent in, sent back, **queried,** lost, found, subjected to public inquiry, lost again, and finally buried in soft peat for three months and recycled as firelighters. On no account should you allow a Vogon to read poetry to you.

Movie: _____

Scene: _____

Bureaucratic might mean _____

_____

Officious might mean _____

_____

Callous might mean _____

_____

Ravenous might mean _____

_____

Queried might mean _____

_____

Hint: The answer to the Ultimate Question of Life, the Universe, and Everything is 42.

Solutions

Let's see how you did. Check your answers and write the exact definitions. To help you memorize the vocabulary words, reread the movie excerpt or even act out the scene with a friend.

Movie: *The Hitchhiker's Guide to the Galaxy,* Touchstone Pictures, 2005

Scene: In this excerpt, the book tells Arthur Dent (Martin Freeman) about Vogons after he and Ford Prefect (played by Mos Def) hitch a ride on a Vogon ship. Arthur and Ford are about to be read Vogon poetry, widely considered the third-worst poetry in the galaxy.

Bureaucratic means *using excessively complicated rules of procedure.*

Officious means *annoyingly interfering and domineering.* Synonyms: bumptious, meddlesome, overbearing, overzealous.

Callous means *insensitive*—the kind of people who would not lift a finger to save their own grandmothers from the Bug-Blatter Beast of Traal!

Ravenous means *famished,* which is why you don't want to leave the ravenous Beast alone with Grandma. Synonyms: gluttonous, greedy, insatiable, voracious.

Queried means *questioned.* This word always makes me think of Tucker's response, "Good **query,** Mary" to a **question** that Mary asked in the hilarious movie *There's Something About Mary.* That movie is the granddaddy of all raucous romantic comedies like *Knocked Up* and *Forgetting Sarah Marshall.* It invented the *genre* (category). If you haven't seen it, check it out. Watch for the zipper scene! Ouch, "Franks and beans!"

Group 69

Here are four one-liners from a movie. See if you can name the movie, describe the scenes, and define the boldface vocabulary words. Check your answers on the following page.

RICKY BOBBY: I'm so proud of you boys. You remind me of me, **precocious** and full of wonderment.

———————————

CAL NAUGHTON, JR.: So when you say **psychosomatic,** you mean like he could start a fire with his thoughts?

———————————

WALKER: Anarchy!

TEXAS RANGER: I don't even know what that means, but I love it!

———————————

TEXAS RANGER: Well, if it isn't our old, mangy, **transient** grandfather.

Movie: _____

Scenes: _____

_____

Precocious might mean _____

Psychosomatic might mean _____

Anarchy might mean _____

Transient might mean _____

Hint: Gary Cole plays Ricky Bobby's father, Reese Bobby. You might also remember him from *Pineapple Express,* where he played drug kingpin Ted Jones.

Solutions

Let's see how you did. Check your answers and write the exact definitions. To help you memorize the vocabulary words, reread the movie excerpts or even act out the scenes with a friend.

Movie: *Talladega Nights: The Ballad of Ricky Bobby,* Columbia Pictures, 2006

Scenes: The first excerpt is from the dinner scene when Ricky Bobby (Will Ferrell) delivers his "little baby Jesus" version of grace before dinner. The second scene is when Cal (John C. Reilly) is at the hospital, after Ricky's accident, asking the doctor if Ricky Bobby will drive again. The third occurs after Ricky Bobby's mom decides to civilize Ricky Bobby's kids (named "Walker" and "Texas Ranger," after the 1990s television show *Walker, Texas Ranger*), and the fourth scene is toward the end of the movie when Reese is waiting for Ricky and family after the final race of the movie.

Precocious means *mature at an early age*. *Pre-* means *before,* which makes sense for *precocious* (mature **before** usual).

Psychosomatic refers to *physical illnesses that are actually caused by the mind.* After Cal inquires about Ricky's health, the doctor answers Cal's question and defines *psychosomatic,* "No, not at all, it means *it's all in his mind.*" When Will Ferrell and Adam McKay wrote this script they must have been planning to help you increase your SAT score! *Psycho-* means *of the mind* and *somatic* means *of the body.* So *psychosomatic* refers to *illnesses **of the body** that are actually **of the mind,*** like Ricky Bobby's belief that he cannot walk or feel his legs—which, being a true friend, Cal disproves by stabbing Ricky Bobby in the leg with a steak knife.

Anarchy means *disorder* or *the absence of law.* Synonyms: bedlam, chaos, mayhem, pandemonium, turmoil. You saw *anarchy* as a synonym for *chaos* in Group 49, which quoted Susan's inspirational speech to Ricky Bobby (just before she got up on the table and started meowing at him).

Transient in this case means *wandering.* Synonym: itinerant. The word *transient* also means *temporary,* which makes sense since a *transient* (wanderer) moves around and is a *transitory* (temporary) visitor, just like the boys' grandfather in the movie, who is repeatedly in and out of their lives.

Group 70

Here's an excerpt from a movie. See if you can name the movie, describe the scene, and define the boldface vocabulary words. Check your answers on the following page.

DEAN PRITCHARD: Topic #1: What is your position on the role of government in supporting **innovation** in the field of biotechnology?

JAMES CARVILLE: Well Dean . . . I'm, I'm glad that you asked that question . . .

FRANK: Uhhh . . . actually, I'd like to jump in and take that one Jimmy, if you don't mind.

JAMES CARVILLE: Have at it, Hoss.

FRANK: Recent research has shown that **empirical** evidence for globalization of corporate innovation is very limited and as a **corollary** the market for technologies is shrinking. As a world leader, it's important for America to provide **systematic** research grants for our scientists. I believe strongly there will always be a need for us to have a well-**articulated** innovation policy with emphasis on human resource development. Thank you.

(Frank grunts, makes a face, and goes limp. The audience applauds.)

Movie: _____

Scene: _____

Innovation might mean _____

Empirical might mean _____

Corollary might mean _____

Systematic might mean _____

Articulated might mean _____

Hint: "Frank the Tank!"

Solutions

Let's see how you did. Check your answers and write the exact definitions. To help you memorize the vocabulary words, reread the movie excerpt or even act out the scene with a friend.

Movie: *Old School,* DreamWorks, 2003

Scene: After the Dean (played by Jeremy Piven of *Entourage*) shuts down the Frat and revokes their charter, Mitch (Luke Wilson) discovers that they can bypass his *injunction* (formal order) by completing a charter review—a series of academic, athletic, and community-service events. Frank's (Will Ferrell) inspired quote is during the debate portion of the charter review.

Inside Scoop: Ellen Pompeo plays Nicole, the woman Mitch has a crush on. When *Old School* came out in 2003, she was not well known, but now everyone knows her as Dr. Meredith Grey on *Grey's Anatomy!* You might also recognize Mitch's boss at the law firm as none other than "Man of Faith" John Locke (Terry O'Quinn) of *Lost!*

Innovation means *change* or *breakthroughs.* Synonym: ingenuity.

Empirical means *observed or experienced, rather than theorized.* Synonym: heuristic.

Corollary means *offshoot* or *consequence,* and was a synonym for *ramification* on the *Batman Begins* page.

Systematic means *with a system—organized.* Synonym: methodical.

Articulated means *communicated.* Do you remember in which movie you learned this word? Answer: In *American Pie* (Group 1), Jim said, "I should be able to talk to girls. I'm **articulate** . . ." That was right before he did unspeakable things with a fresh-baked apple pie.

Quiz 7

I. Let's review some of the words that you've seen in Groups 61–70. Match each of the following words to the correct definition or synonym on the right. If you need help, refer back to the movie excerpts and definitions. Then check the solutions on page 234.

1. Fabrication	A. Sovereign
2. Erroneous	B. Immoderate
3. Dogma	C. Anger
4. Autonomous	D. Entreat
5. Umbrage	E. Prevarication
6. Verisimilitude	F. Aberrations
7. Implore	G. Creed
8. Incontrovertible	H. Specious
9. Thwart	I. Credibility
10. Comely	J. Clandestine
11. Intemperate	K. Mutually beneficial
12. Arduous	L. Indubitable
13. Symbiotic	M. Herculean
14. Covert	N. Pulchritudinous
15. Anomalies	O. Stymie

II. Let's review several of the word parts that you've seen in Groups 61–70. Match each of the following word parts to the correct definition or synonym on the right. Then check the solutions on page 234.

16. –ous (as in *erroneous*)	A. Not
17. Auto- (as in *autonomous*)	B. Of the mind
18. In- (as in *incontrovertible*)	C. Characterized by
19. Sym- (as in *symbiotic*)	D. Before
20. Psycho- (as in *psychosomatic*)	E. Together
21. Pre- (as in *precocious*)	F. Self

Quiz 7 (continued)

III. Match each group of synonyms to its general meaning. Then check the solutions on page 234.

22. Erroneous
    Fallacious
    Specious

23. Beseech
    Entreat
    Implore
    Importune

24. Forestall
    Stonewall
    Stymie
    Thwart

25. Arduous
    Herculean
    Laborious
    Onerous
    Toilsome

26. Comely
    Fair
    Fetching
    Prepossessing
    Pulchritudinous

27. Aberrations
    Anomalies
    Incongruities

A. Attractive

B. Irregularities

C. Difficult

D. Beg

E. Incorrect

F. Prevent

Group 71

Here's an excerpt from a movie. See if you can name the movie, describe the scene, and define the boldface vocabulary word. Check your answers on the following page.

A.D.: You need a shave, my friend. You know, at times I forget how much you've grown. At times, I still see the small boy from the cupboard. Forgive my **mawkishness,** . . . I am an old man.

Movie: _____

Scene: _____

_____

Mawkishness might mean _____

_____

Hint: " . . . is who I need. Wake him. Tell him what happened. Speak to no one else . . . (*They hear someone coming.*) Hide yourself below, Harry. Don't speak or be seen by anybody without my permission. Whatever happens, it is *imperative* you stay below. Harry, do as I say. Trust me. Trust me."

Solutions

Let's see how you did. Check your answers and write the exact definition. To help you memorize the vocabulary word, reread the movie excerpt or even act out the scene with a friend.

Movie: *Harry Potter and the Half-Blood Prince,* Warner Bros., 2009

Scene: As Harry (Daniel Radcliffe) is walking toward Dumbledore in the Hogwarts' clock tower, he overhears Professor Snape (Alan Rickman) and Dumbledore (Michael Gambon) arguing. Harry approaches Dumbledore, who speaks these lines.

Vocabulary in the Hint: *Imperative* means *critically important.* Synonym: vital.

Mawkishness means *emotional sappiness.* Why is Dumbledore feeling **emotionally sappy?** It has to do with the conversation he just had with Snape; he knows what's coming . . . Synonyms for *mawkish:* cloying, overly sentimental, saccharine, treacly. The word *treacly* stumped nearly everyone on a recent SAT—everyone except people who recognized the connection to Harry Potter's favorite **sweet and sappy** desert, **treacle** tart!

Group 72

Here's an excerpt from a movie. See if you can name the movie, describe the scene, and define the boldface vocabulary words. Check your answers on the following page.

OPTIMUS: General, our alliance has **countermanded** six Decepticon **incursions** this year, each on a different continent . . .

NATIONAL SECURITY ADVISER: Excuse me! With this . . . so-called "All Spark" now destroyed, why hasn't the enemy left the planet like you thought they would? . . . And the newest members of your team. I understand they arrived here after you sent a message into space. An open invitation . . . "Come to Earth" . . . **vetted** by no one at the White House.

GENERAL: Let me stop you right there, Mr. Galloway. It was vetted right here. And in my experience the judgment of both Major Lenox and his team has always been above **reproach.**

Movie: _____

Scene: _____

Countermanded might mean _____

_____

Incursions might mean _____

_____

Vetted might mean _____

_____

Reproach might mean _____

_____

Hint: "Dad, whoa! I'm watching what you're doing, Dad! It's not a rap video."

Solutions

Let's see how you did. Check your answers and write the exact definitions. To help you memorize the vocabulary words, reread the movie excerpt or even act out the scene with a friend.

Movie: *Transformers: Revenge of the Fallen,* DreamWorks, 2009

Scene: The Autobots (alien robots working with the U.S. military) and U.S. Special Forces are reporting to the General after returning from a battle in Shanghai. They are interrupted by the President's National Security Advisor, Mr. Galloway. He does not know that they are being bugged by the Decepticons (a group of hostile alien robots) and spills the beans to the locations of Megatron and the All-Spark shard (a very powerful device that grants life to machines).

Inside Scoop: Apparently, Megan Fox's favorite Transformer is Devastator (a massive Decepticon formed from construction vehicles), and Shia LaBeouf's favorite is Scalpel (the small Decepticon that begins to examine Sam while he is captured).

Countermanded means *reversed, cancelled,* or *stopped. Counter-* means *against* and *-mand* implies *command,* so *countermand* means *against the command—reverse, cancel, or stop* something, such as an *incursion* (attack). Synonyms: abrogated, annulled, nullified, quashed, repealed, rescinded, revoked, voided.

Incursions means *attacks.* Synonyms: forays, sorties.

Vetted means *carefully examined.* Synonym: scrutinized.

Reproach means *blame or scolding,* so *above reproach* means *above scolding—perfect.* Synonyms: admonishment, censure, rebuke, reprimand, reproof.

Group 73

Here's an excerpt from a movie. See if you can name the movie, describe the scene, and define the boldface vocabulary words. Check your answers on the following page.

FLETCHER REEDE: He's a **pedantic, pontificating, pretentious** bastard; a **belligerent** old fart; a worthless, steaming pile of cow dung, **figuratively** speaking . . .

MR. ALLEN: I like your style, Reede! That's just what this stuffy company needs—a little **irreverence!**

Movie: _____

Scene: _____

Pedantic might mean _____

_____

Pontificating might mean _____

_____

Pretentious might mean _____

_____

Belligerent might mean _____

_____

Figuratively might mean _____

_____

Irreverence might mean _____

_____

Hint #1: "I wish that for only one day Dad couldn't tell a lie."
Hint #2: Jim Carrey

Solutions

Let's see how you did. Check your answers and write the exact definitions. To help you memorize the vocabulary words, reread the movie excerpt or even act out the scene with a friend.

Movie: *Liar Liar,* Universal Pictures, 1997

Scene: Fletcher Reede (Jim Carrey) is a lawyer who lies all the time . . . at work, in court, and to his family. His son, Max, wishes on his birthday that his dad can no longer lie. Magically it works, and that gets Jim Carrey's character into lots of trouble, such as when he is asked what he really thinks of his boss, Mr. Allen.

Pedantic means *annoyingly precise*. Synonyms: captious, fastidious, finicky, fussy, meticulous, perfectionist, persnickety, punctilious, scrupulous.

Pontificating means *annoyingly preachy*. Synonym: dogmatizing.

Pretentious means *snobby, showy, or conceited, especially in an attempt to impress*. Remember from earlier in this book that Juno was called "pretentious" for judging the name "Madison" (Group 47). Synonyms: affected, ostentatious, pompous. Standardized tests love to use these words. Remember to say or write *pretentious* and its synonyms five times—it's a great way to memorize a bunch of high-level vocabulary words all at one time.

Belligerent means *hostile*. Synonyms: bellicose, inimical, pugnacious, truculent.

Figuratively means *not literally (metaphorically)*. Synonym: allegorically.

Irreverence means *disrespect and lack of seriousness*. Synonyms: contempt, flippancy, impertinence, impudence, insolence.

Let's translate this excerpt using the definitions from above:

FLETCHER REEDE: He's an **annoyingly precise, preachy, snobby** bastard; a hostile old fart; a worthless, steaming pile of cow dung, **metaphorically** speaking . . .

MR. ALLEN: I like your style, Reede! That's just what this stuffy company needs—a little **disrespect and lack of seriousness!**

Group 74

Here are two excerpts from a movie. See if you can name the movie, describe the scenes, and define the boldface vocabulary words. Check your answers on the following page.

BRENNAN: Listen, I know that we started out as **foe,** but after that courageous act that you showed me against the one they call Derek, maybe someday we could become friends, . . . friends who ride **majestic translucent** steeds, shooting flaming arrows across the Bridge of Hemdale.

———————

BRENNAN: Mom, Doback, we think it would be very **prudent** . . .

DALE: Can we turn our beds into bunk beds?

BRENNAN: . . . And here's the thing, it would give us so much extra space in our room to do activities.

DALE: Please say "yes."

Movie: _____

Scenes: _____

_____

Foe might mean _____

Majestic might mean _____

Translucent might mean _____

Prudent might mean _____

Hint: "This is gonna sound weird, but for a second, I think you took on the shape of a unicorn."

Solutions

Let's see how you did. Check your answers and write the exact definitions. To help you memorize the vocabulary words, reread the movie excerpts or even act out the scenes with a friend.

Movie: *Step Brothers,* Columbia Pictures, 2008

Scenes: Brennan (Will Ferrell) is thirty-nine years old and lives with his mother. Dale (John C. Reilly) is forty years old and lives with his father. When their parents marry, Brennan and Dale become step brothers and must share a room in their new home. In the first excerpt, Brennan and Dale end their feud and become friends after Dale punches Brennan's brother, Derek (Adam Scott). In the second excerpt, Brennan and Dale ask their parents for permission to convert their beds into bunk beds.

Foe means *enemy.*

Majestic means *beautiful, dignified,* or *regal.* Synonyms: august, distinguished, noble, resplendent, stately, sumptuous.

Translucent means *allowing light but not images through,* like through frosted glass you can see light but not clear images. *Translucent* is an interesting word to break apart. *Trans-* means *through* or *across, luc* implies *light* (like *luz* in Spanish), and *-ent* can mean *occurrence.* That's why *translucent* means the **occurrence** of **light** going **through.**

Prudent means *sensible, especially with regard to future outcomes.* If you've ever seen *Saturday Night Live* reruns of Dana Carvey impersonating George H. W. Bush, then you've heard him say "prudent." Former President Bush was famous for using this word a lot. Synonyms: astute, judicious, sagacious, shrewd. Standardized tests love to use an antonym for *prudent: myopic*—it means *shortsighted, not thinking about the future.*

Group 75

Here's an excerpt from a movie. See if you can name the movie, describe the scene, and define the boldface vocabulary words. Check your answers on the following page.

Look at me. Judge me by my size, do you? Hmm? Hmm . . . And well you should not. For my ally is the Force, and a powerful ally it is. Life creates it, makes it grow. Its energy surrounds us and binds us. **Luminous** beings are we, not this **crude** matter. You must feel the Force around you; here, between you, me, the tree, the rock, everywhere, yes. Even between the land and the ship.

Movie: _____

Scene: _____

_____

Luminous might mean _____

_____

Crude might mean _____

_____

Hint: "Do . . . or do not. There is no try."

Solutions

Let's see how you did. Check your answers and write the exact definitions. To help you memorize the vocabulary words, reread the movie excerpt or even act out the scene with a friend.

Movie: *Star Wars Episode V: The Empire Strikes Back,* 20th Century Fox, 1980

Scene: I had to leave out the name of the character for this quote; Yoda would have been too much of a giveaway! Luke Skywalker (Mark Hamill) has found Yoda on the planet Dagobah, where Yoda will teach Luke to use the Force in his Jedi training. Luke doubts his ability to raise a ship out of the swamp, so Yoda dishes out some wisdom.

Luminous means *radiant.* Yoda means that we are spiritual beings, permeated by the Force, not just crude skin and bones. Yoda gives a mighty fine motivational speech.

Crude means *simple, vulgar,* or *unrefined,* as in **crude** (simple) tools of the Stone Age, **crude** (vulgar) jokes in the movie *Knocked Up,* and **crude** (unrefined) oil.

Group 76

Here's an excerpt from a movie. See if you can name the movie, describe the scene, and define the boldface vocabulary words. Check your answers on the following page.

SPOCK: You are, in fact, the Mr. Scott who **postulated** the theory of transwarp beaming?

SCOTTY: That's what I'm talkin' about! How do you think I wound up here? Had a little debate with my instructor on the issue of **relativistic** physics and how it pertains to subspace travel . . . I told him that I could not only beam a grapefruit from one planet to the adjacent planet in the same system—which is easy, by the way—I could do it with a life form. So, I tested it out on Admiral Archer's prized beagle.

KIRK: Wait, I know that dog. What happened to it?

SCOTTY: I'll tell you when it reappears . . . Ahem. I don't know, I do feel guilty about that . . . So, the Enterprise has had its **maiden** voyage, has it? She is one well-**endowed** lady. I'd like to get my hands on her "ample **nacelles**," if you pardon the engineering **parlance** . . .

Movie: _____

Scene: _____

Postulated might mean _____

Relativistic might mean _____

Maiden might mean _____

Endowed might mean _____

Nacelles might mean _____

Parlance might mean _____

Hint: "I'm giving her all she's got, Captain!"

Solutions

Let's see how you did. Check your answers and write the exact definitions. To help you memorize the vocabulary words, reread the movie excerpt or even act out the scene with a friend.

Movie: *Star Trek,* Paramount Pictures, 2009

Scene: Kirk (Chris Pine) and future Spock (Leonard Nimoy) meet young Scotty (Simon Pegg) who has been exiled to a remote outpost. Soon after they are reunited, Scotty gets to give his classic line, "I'm giving her all she's got, Captain!"

Postulated means *suggested.* Synonyms: hypothesized, posited, proposed.

Relativistic means *not set, but **related** to other factors,* so the term *relativistic physics,* in the excerpt, refers to *the theory that physical properties, such as mass and length, are **not set, but affected by** the speed that an object is moving.*

Maiden in this case means *first.* Synonyms: inaugural, virgin. *Maiden* can also mean *unmarried* or *pertaining to a young woman.*

Endowed means *equipped* or *blessed.* Scotty means that the ship is well-**equipped**—it has state-of-the-art systems, weapons, etc . . .

Nacelles means *streamlined casings (material that encloses) of an engine, or warp engine in this case.* I think Scotty has been on a remote base for way too long and has taken this sexual innuendo a bit too far!

Parlance in this case means *slang.* Synonym: jargon.

Group 77

Here's an excerpt from a movie. See if you can name the movie, describe the scene, and define the boldface vocabulary words. Check your answers on the following page.

JARVIS: A very **astute** observation, sir . . .

TONY: Use the gold-titanium **alloy** from the **Seraphim** tactical satellite. That should ensure **fuselage integrity** while maintaining power-to-weight ratio. Got it?

JARVIS: Yes. Shall I **render** using proposed specifications?

TONY: Thrill me.

JARVIS: The render is complete.

TONY: (*sees the new design on a computer screen*) A little **ostentatious,** don't you think?

JARVIS: What was I thinking? You're usually so **discreet.**

TONY: Tell you what. Throw a little hot-rod red in there.

JARVIS: Yes, that should help you keep a low profile. The render is complete.

TONY: Hey, I like it. **Fabricate** it. Paint it.

JARVIS: **Commencing** automated assembly.

Movie: _____

Scene: _____

_____

Hint: This film stars the actor who plays Kirk Lazarus in *Tropic Thunder*.

Group 77 (continued)

Astute might mean _____

_____

Alloy might mean _____

_____

Seraphim might mean _____

_____

Fuselage might mean _____

_____

Integrity might mean _____

_____

Render might mean _____

_____

Ostentatious might mean _____

_____

Discreet might mean _____

_____

Fabricate might mean _____

_____

Commencing might mean _____

_____

Solutions

Let's see how you did. Check your answers and write the exact definitions. To help you memorize the vocabulary words, reread the movie excerpt or even act out the scene with a friend.

Movie: *Iron Man,* Paramount Pictures, 2008

Scene: Tony (Robert Downey, Jr.) is designing the Iron Man suit with the help of his trusty computer, Jarvis (voiced by Paul Bettany). Tony and his computers have a pretty funny *repartee* (banter, wordplay), especially earlier in the movie when the robot named "Dummy" keeps dousing Tony as though he is on fire during tests of the suit. Tony gets mad and says, "If you douse me again, and I'm not on fire, I'm donating you to a city college . . . "

Inside Scoop: Rap artist Ghostface Killah is a fan of the *Iron Man* comics and scored a cameo as a Dubaian businessman. His scene was cut from the final movie, but *Iron Man*'s director, Jon Favreau, apologized to Ghostface and used his "We Celebrate" video in the movie.

Astute means *intelligent and insightful*. Synonyms: canny, incisive, judicious, keen, perspicacious, sagacious, savvy, shrewd, wise.

Alloy means *mixture*. Synonyms: amalgam, composite, fusion.

Seraphim means *angel*. In this case, it is also the name of a *tactical* (strategic) satellite. Synonym: cherubim.

Fuselage means *outer covering of a vehicle or device*.

Integrity in this case means *durability*. It can also mean *honesty*.

Render in this case means *create*.

Ostentatious means *showy*. Synonyms: brash, flamboyant, gaudy, ornate, pretentious, vulgar.

Discreet means *inconspicuous*. Synonyms: chary, circumspect, prudent, understated, unobtrusive. *Discreet* can also mean *tactful (sensitive in dealing with others)*.

Fabricate means *construct*. Notice that *render* in this excerpt means **create a picture of it on the screen,** and *fabricate* means **construct** *the actual suit*.

Commencing means *beginning*.

Group 78

Here's an excerpt from a movie. See if you can name the movie, describe the scene, and define the boldface vocabulary words. Check your answers on the following page.

ELLERBY: This is a new unit, and you are the newest members of it. You have been selected for it on the basis of intelligence and **aptitude.** This is an **elite** unit. Our job is to smash, or **marginally** disrupt, organized crime in the city by **enhanced** cooperation with the FBI, represented here today by Agent Frank Lazio. And we will do it. By organized crime in this city, you know who we mean. That's Jackie Costigan. That's an old picture. Jackie met his **demise.**

Movie: _____

Scene: _____
_____

Aptitude might mean _____
_____

Elite might mean _____
_____

Marginally might mean _____
_____

Enhanced might mean _____
_____

Demise might mean _____
_____

Hint: This movie featured Leonardo DiCaprio, Matt Damon, Jack Nicholson, Mark Wahlberg, Martin Sheen, and Alec Baldwin.

Solutions

Let's see how you did. Check your answers and write the exact definitions. To help you memorize the vocabulary words, reread the movie excerpt or even act out the scene with a friend.

Movie: *The Departed,* Warner Bros., 2006

Scene: Ellerby (Alec Baldwin) is showing slides and introducing the police officers to their new assignment: organized crime boss Frank Costello (Jack Nicholson).

Inside Scoop: Although Nicholson plays a Boston, Massachusetts, crime boss, he refused to wear a Boston Red Sox hat during filming and instead wore his New York Yankees cap!

Aptitude means *talent.* Synonym: faculty.

Elite means *cream of the crop* or *the best.* Synonym: nonpareil.

Marginally means *slightly.*

Enhanced means *increased* or *improved.*

Demise means *destruction* or *death.* Synonyms: expiry, quietus.

Here's an excerpt from a movie. See if you can name the movie, describe the scene, and define the boldface vocabulary words. Check your answers on the following page.

CHARLIE MACKENZIE: (*reciting a poem that he wrote to win back his girlfriend after they had a fight*)

> Harriet.
> Harry-ette.
> Hard-hearted **harbinger** of **haggis.**
> Beautiful, **bemuse-ed, bellicose** butcher.
> Un-trust . . . ing.
> Un-know . . . ing.
> Un-love . . . ed?
> "He wants you back," he screamed into the night air like a fireman going to a window that has no fire . . . except the passion of his heart.

Movie: _____

Scene: _____

_____

Harbinger might mean _____

_____

Haggis might mean _____

_____

Bemused might mean _____

_____

Bellicose might mean _____

_____

Hint: Charlie MacKenzie is played by the same actor who plays Austin Powers.

Solutions

Let's see how you did. Check your answers and write the exact definitions. To help you memorize the vocabulary words, reread the movie excerpt or even act out the scene with a friend.

Movie: *So I Married an Axe Murderer,* TriStar Pictures, 1993

Scene: If you are a Mike Myers (*Austin Powers, Shrek, Wayne's World*) fan, then this oldie but goodie is a *must*-see. In this scene, Charlie (Mike Myers) is serenading his girlfriend, Harriet (Nancy Travis), with a love poem.

Inside Scoop: Did you notice Mike Myers in a more serious role in Quentin Tarantino's *Inglourious Basterds?* He played General Ed Fenech, whom Tarantino named after the Italian sex-comedy actress, Edwige Fenech.

Harbinger means *something that signals the approach of something else.* Harriet works in a Scottish butcher shop, so she serves up oodles of tasty haggis; that's why Charlie calls her a "harbinger of haggis." Synonyms: augury, forerunner, foretoken, forewarning, herald, indication, omen, portent, precursor, presage.

Haggis refers to (wait for it . . .) *sheep's intestines and organs mixed with fat, oatmeal, and seasoning, and then boiled in the sheep's stomach.* Yum. Synonyms: there are no synonyms for that!

Bemused means *confused.* Synonyms: bewildered, flummoxed, nonplussed.

Bellicose means *aggressive or warlike.* Synonyms: antagonistic, belligerent, contentious, hawkish, inimical, pugnacious, truculent.

Group 80

Here are two excerpts from a movie. See if you can name the movie, describe the scenes, and define the boldface vocabulary words. Check your answers on the following page.

PHIL: You're not really wearing that are you?

ALAN: Wearing what?

PHIL: The man purse. You're *actually* gonna wear that . . . ?

ALAN: It's where I keep all my things. I get a lot of compliments on this. Plus, it's not a man purse, it's called a **satchel.** Indiana Jones wears one.

———————

STU: Hey Phil, am I missing a tooth? . . . (*Holds up a shiny tray that was on the coffee table so he can see his tooth.*) Oh. My. God! My **lateral incisor,** it's gone!

PHIL: OK, OK, OK, we just need to calm down, we're fine. Everything's fine. Alan, go wake up Doug. Let's get some coffee . . .

ALAN: Hey guys, he's not in there.

Movie: _____

Scenes: _____

_____

Satchel might mean _____

Lateral might mean _____

Incisor might mean _____

Hint: "I tend to think of myself as a one-man wolf pack. But when my sister brought Doug home, I knew he was one of my own. And my wolf pack . . . it grew by one."

Solutions

Let's see how you did. Check your answers and write the exact definitions. To help you memorize the vocabulary words, reread the movie excerpts or even act out the scenes with a friend.

Movie: *The Hangover,* Warner Bros., 2009

Scenes: Before the first excerpt, Alan (Zach Galifianakis) says, "Hey guys, you ready to let the dogs out?" and then does his little dance. The music starts, and the guys head to the elevator where Phil (Bradley Cooper) notices Alan's man purse, er . . . satchel. In the second excerpt, the guys wake up and discover their plight: the villa is trashed, there's a tiger in the bathroom, Stu is missing a tooth, and Doug is missing completely.

Inside Scoop: Ed Helms, who plays Stu, is actually missing his **lateral incisor** (he usually wears an artificial implant) and did not require props or CGI (computer-generated imagery) to make it look like he was missing the tooth!

Satchel means *a bag that is carried by a long strap over the shoulder.* Synonyms: man purse, murse (just kidding).

Lateral means *on the side* or *sideways.*

Incisor refers to a *sharp tooth in the front of the mouth,* so a *lateral incisor* is a *sharp tooth on the side of the front of the mouth.* The word part *cis-* implies *cut* as in *incision* (a surgical **cut**), and can help you remember words like *concise* (lots of information **cut** down to what's most important—succinct), *incisive* (**cutting** right to the core of an issue—sharp-witted and astute), and *exorcise* (**cut** out an evil spirit—expel).

Quiz 8

I. Let's review some of the words that you've seen in Groups 71–80. Match each of the following words to the correct definition or synonym on the right. If you need help, refer back to the movie excerpts and definitions. Then check the solutions on page 234.

1. Imperative
2. Mawkish
3. Countermand
4. Vetted
5. Reproach
6. Pedantic
7. Belligerent
8. Irreverent
9. Majestic
10. Postulate
11. Parlance
12. Astute
13. Ostentatious
14. Discreet
15. Harbinger

A. Abrogate
B. Admonish
C. Jargon
D. Vital
E. Pretentious
F. Canny
G. Circumspect
H. Saccharine
I. Portent
J. Fastidious
K. Posit
L. Truculent
M. Scrutinized
N. August
O. Insolent

II. Let's review several of the word parts that you've seen in Groups 71–80. Match each of the following word parts to the correct definition or synonym on the right. Then check the solutions on page 234.

16. Counter- (as in *countermand*)
17. -mand (as in *countermand*)
18. Cis- (as in *incisor*)
Review from earlier groups:
19. Lumin- (as in *luminous*)
20. Equiv- (as in *equivocal*)
21. A- (as in *anomaly*)

A. Command
B. Light
C. Not
D. Equal
E. Against
F. Cut

183

Quiz 8 (continued)

III. Match each group of synonyms to its general meaning. Then check the solutions on page 234.

22. Cloying
    Mawkish
    Saccharine
    Treacly

    A. Precise

23. Admonish
    Censure
    Rebuke
    Reprimand
    Reproach
    Reproof

    B. Aggressive

24. Flippancy
    Impertinence
    Impudence
    Insolence
    Irreverence

    C. Scold

25. Captious
    Fastidious
    Meticulous
    Pedantic
    Punctilious
    Scrupulous

    D. Forewarning

26. Augury
    Harbinger
    Omen
    Portent
    Presage

    E. Disrespect

27. Bellicose
    Belligerent
    Inimical
    Pugnacious
    Truculent

    F. Sappy

Group 81

Here's an excerpt from a movie. See if you can name the movie, describe the scene, and define the boldface vocabulary word. Check your answers on the following page.

RICHIE: This is the newly formed Essex County Narcotics Squad. Our **mandate** is to make major arrests, no street guys. We're looking for the suppliers and the distributors . . .

JONES: I heard a story about you: that you found a million dollars in unmarked cash and you gave that . . . back. Is that true?

RICHIE: Yeah, I did. Anybody got a problem with that?

Movie: _____

Scene: _____

_____

Mandate might mean _____

_____

Hint: In 2007, Jay-Z released an album with the same name as this movie.

Solutions

Let's see how you did. Check your answers and write the exact definition. To help you memorize the vocabulary word, reread the movie excerpt or even act out the scene with a friend.

Movie: *American Gangster,* Universal Pictures, 2007

Scene: Richie (Russell Crowe) has been appointed to assemble and manage a new Essex County Narcotics Squad.

Inside Scoop: *American Gangster* is based on the true stories of Frank Lucas and Richie Roberts, and for accuracy in the film, Frank Lucas and Richie Roberts were on set to consult with Denzel Washington, Russell Crowe, and director Ridley Scott during production of the film.

Mandate means *formal order,* like *mandato* in Spanish, which means *command.* If you're a fan of *Monty Python and the Holy Grail,* you might remember the hilarious line that Dennis delivers to King Arthur when they are discussing why Arthur is King, "Listen, strange women lyin' in ponds distributin' swords is no basis for a system of government. Supreme executive power derives from a **mandate** from the masses, not from some farcical aquatic ceremony." Synonyms: decree, directive, edict, fiat, injunction, proclamation.

Group 82

Here are two excerpts from a movie. See if you can name the movie, describe the scenes, and define the boldface vocabulary words. Check your answers on the following page.

STUDENT: Excuse me, Dr. Jones. I just had a question on Hardgrove's **normative** culture model.

DR. JONES: Forget Hardgrove. Read Vere Gordon Childe on **diffusionism.** He spent most of his life in the field. If you want to be a good archaeologist, you've got to get out of the library.

———

JONES: You're pulling against a **vacuum.** It's like trying to lift a car. Just stay calm.

MARION: Okay, I'm calm.

MUTT: What is it? Quicksand?

JONES: No. It's a dry sandpit. Quicksand is a mix of sand, mud, and water, and depending on the **viscosity,** it's not as dangerous as people sometimes think.

MARION: Oh, for Pete's sake, Jones, we're not in school.

JONES: Don't worry. There's nothing to worry about unless there's a . . . (*Marion and Jones start sinking into the dry sand pit.*) **void** collapse . . .

MUTT: I'll go get something to pull you up . . .

MARION: Mutt can be a little **impetuous.**

JONES: Ah, it's not the worse quality in the world.

Movie: _____

Scenes: _____

_____

Hint: For his role as Mutt, Shia LaBeouf gained fifteen pounds of muscle.

Group 82 (continued)

Normative might mean _____

_____

Diffusionism might mean _____

_____

Vacuum might mean _____

_____

Viscosity might mean _____

_____

Void might mean _____

_____

Impetuous might mean _____

_____

Solutions

Let's see how you did. Check your answers and write the exact definitions. To help you memorize the vocabulary words, reread the movie excerpts or even act out the scenes with a friend.

Movie: *Indiana Jones and the Kingdom of the Crystal Skull*, Paramount Pictures, 2008

Scenes: In the first excerpt, Indiana Jones (Harrison Ford) and Mutt (Shia LaBeouf) have just crashed through the library during a chase scene, and a student asks Indy a question. In the second excerpt, while Indy and the group are evading capture, Indy and Marion realize that they are standing on a sandpit.

Inside Scoop: There are a lot of references in this movie to Indy's advanced age. Interestingly, hoping to help Americans overcome their fear of aging, Harrison Ford requested that the age jokes be added to the script. You go, Harrison Ford! He can still kick butt at any age!

Solutions (continued)

Normative means *relating to what is the norm,* and the *norm* means *something that is typical or standard,* so *normative* means *relating to what is typical or standard.* Synonyms for *norm:* convention, exemplar.

Diffusionism refers to the *theory that similarities between cultures have been **diffused** (spread) from one culture to another. Diffuse* can also mean *wordy* which is a great chance to review synonyms for *wordy:* circumlocutory, digressive, discursive, effusive, garrulous, loquacious, periphrastic, prolix, and verbose, many of which you learned from John Cusack in *Con Air* (Group 57).

Vacuum refers to a *completely empty space* and comes from the Latin word *vacuus,* meaning *empty.* That reminds me of the high-level standardized test word *vacuous,* which means *mindless* or *empty.* You learned *vacuous* from *Zoolander* (Group 7): "We need an empty vessel . . . a shallow, dumb, **vacuous** moron." Synonyms for *vacuous:* fatuous, inane, insipid, vacant, vapid.

Viscosity means *gooeyness.*

Void means a *completely empty space.* Synonym: vacuum.

Impetuous means *spontaneous and impulsive.* Synonyms: hasty, heedless, imprudent, precipitate, rash, temerarious, unpremeditated.

Group 83

Here are a bunch of lines from a movie. See if you can name the movie and define the boldface vocabulary words. Check your answers on the following page.

RULE #13: Bridesmaids are **desperate**—**console** them.

RULE #31: If you call an **audible,** always make sure your fellow Crashers know.

RULE #46: The Rules of Wedding Crashing are sacred. Don't **sully** them by "improvising."

RULE #50: Be **pensive!** It draws out the "healer" in women.

RULE #82: Always think ahead, but always stay in the moment. **Reconcile** this **paradox** and you'll not only get the girl, you might also get peace of mind.

RULE #99: Be **judicious** with cologne. Citrus tones are best.

Movie: _____

Desperate might mean _____

Console might mean _____

Audible might mean _____

Sully might mean _____

Pensive might mean _____

Reconcile might mean _____

Paradox might mean _____

Judicious might mean _____

Hint: "Tattoo on the lower back, might as well be a bull's-eye."

Solutions

Let's see how you did. Check your answers and write the exact definitions. To help you memorize the vocabulary words, reread the movie excerpts or even act out the scenes with a friend.

Movie: *Wedding Crashers,* New Line Cinema, 2005

Scenes: These lines are a sampling from the Wedding Crashers' rulebook. You should check out the full list online; they're hilarious! In 2006, *Premiere* magazine voted *Wedding Crashers* one of "The Fifty Greatest Comedies of All Time." I'd put it at least in the top five.

Inside Scoop: Did you recognize Rachel McAdams, John's love interest Claire, as queen bee Regina George, leader of the Plastics clique in *Mean Girls?*

Desperate means *distressed, needy,* or *hopeless.* Synonyms: desolate, forlorn.

Console means *comfort.* Synonym: solace.

Audible in this case means *change of plans.* This term comes from football lingo and refers to a quarterback calling out a **change of play.** *Audible* also means *hearable.* That's the connection, the quarterback **calls out** the change of play—it's hearable.

Sully means *dirty.* Synonyms: befoul, besmirch, blemish, defile, mar, pollute, soil, stain, spoil, taint, tarnish.

Pensive means *introspective* or *thoughtful.* Synonyms: brooding, contemplative, meditative, musing, reflective, ruminative.

Reconcile in this case means *settle,* but it can also mean *reunite.*

Paradox means *contradiction.*

Judicious means *sensible.* *Anchorman's* Brian Fontana (Paul Rudd) could certainly have used a dose of this wisdom. Then he might have avoided clearing the newsroom with the *formidable* (powerful) scent of his Sex Panther cologne, the one that smells like "a turd covered in burnt hair" (Group 40). Synonyms: astute, canny, discerning, percipient, politic, prudent, sagacious, shrewd.

Group 84

Here's an excerpt from a movie. See if you can name the movie, describe the scene, and define the boldface vocabulary words. Check your answers on the following page.

MARCUS AURELIUS: My powers will pass to Maximus, to hold in trust until the Senate is ready to rule once more. Rome is to be a **republic** again.

COMMODUS: Maximus?

MARCUS AURELIUS: Yes. My decision disappoints you?

COMMODUS: You wrote to me once, listing the four chief **virtues:** Wisdom, justice, **fortitude,** and **temperance.** As I read the list, I knew I had none of them. But I have other virtues, Father. Ambition. That can be a virtue when it drives us to excel. **Resourcefulness,** courage, perhaps not on the battlefield, but . . . there are many forms of courage.

Movie: _____

Scene: _____

_____

Republic might mean _____

Virtues might mean _____

Fortitude might mean _____

Temperance might mean _____

Resourcefulness might mean _____

Hint: "Busy . . . little . . . bees."

Solutions

Let's see how you did. Check your answers and write the exact definitions. To help you memorize the vocabulary words, reread the movie excerpt or even act out the scene with a friend.

Movie: *Gladiator,* DreamWorks, 2000

Scene: Roman Emperor Marcus Aurelius (played by Richard Harris, who also played Albus Dumbledore in the first two *Harry Potter* movies) has just asked Maximus (Russell Crowe) to rule Rome after Aurelius dies. In the excerpt, Marcus Aurelius' thoroughly disturbing son, Commodus (Joaquin Phoenix), does not like that decision one little bit.

Republic means *government ruled by its people or by an elected ruler, rather than an all-powerful king, queen, or emperor.* You first learned this word from General Tarkin of *Star Wars Episode IV: A New Hope* (Group 56).

Virtues means *good qualities.* The opposite of *virtue* is *vice,* a *bad quality.*

Fortitude means *courage and strength.* Synonyms: audacity, doggedness, doughtiness, grit, indefatigability, intrepidity, mettle, moxie, perseverance, pertinacity, pluck, resolve, steadfastness, tenacity.

Temperance means *self-restraint.* That's why advocates of The **Temperance** Movement, who believed that people needed to exercise **self-restraint** and abstain from alcohol, championed Prohibition in the United States from 1920 to 1933.

Resourcefulness means *the ability to creatively solve problems*—to use **resources** creatively. Synonyms: enterprise, gumption, ingenuity, initiative, inventiveness.

Group 85

Here's an excerpt from a movie. See if you can name the movie, describe the scene, and define the boldface vocabulary words. Check your answers on the following page.

A starship captain's life is filled with **solemn** duty. I have commanded men in battle. I have negotiated peace treaties between **implacable** enemies. I have represented the **Federation** in first contact with twenty-seven alien species. But none of this compares to my solemn duty today . . . as best man. Now, I know on an occasion such as this it is expected that I be **gracious** and **fulsome** with praise on the wonders of this blessed union, but have the two of you considered what you were doing to me? Of course you're happy. But what about my needs? This is all a damned inconvenience. I mean, while you're happily settling in on the Titan, I will be training my new first officer. You all know him. He's a **tyrannical martinet** who will never ever allow me to go on away missions.

Movie: _____

Scene: _____

_____

Solemn might mean _____

Implacable might mean _____

Federation might mean _____

Gracious might mean _____

Fulsome might mean _____

Tyrannical might mean _____

Martinet might mean _____

Hint: "Make it so, Number One!"

Solutions

Let's see how you did. Check your answers and write the exact definitions. To help you memorize the vocabulary words, reread the movie excerpt or even act out the scene with a friend.

Movie: *Star Trek Nemesis,* Paramount Pictures, 2002

Scene: This is Captain Picard's Best Man toast at the wedding of First Officer William T. Riker and Counselor Deanna Troi. Picard (Patrick Stewart) would make John and Jeremy proud—Wedding Crashers Rule #19: "Toast in the native language if you know the native language and have practiced the toast. Do not wing it."

Solemn means *serious.* Synonyms: earnest, grave, sober, somber.

Implacable means *unstoppable* or *unable to be satisfied.* This actually comes from the word *placate,* meaning *satisfy or soothe.* Since *im-* means *not, implacable* means *not satisfiable.* Synonyms: inexorable, intransigent, relentless, unappeasable.

Federation means *an allied group of states.* Picard is, of course, referring to The United Federation of Planets, also known as "The Federation." *Star Trek* presents "The Federation" as an interstellar federal *polity* (government) with planets and colonies spread throughout the Milky Way galaxy. The Federation is a liberal democracy and constitutional **republic,** though it has also been described as a utopian **socialist** society. Do you remember the words in bold? If not, review *Gladiator's* and Ferris Bueller's political lessons in Groups 84 and 29, respectively.

Gracious means *courteous.* Synonyms: amiable, benevolent, chivalrous, civil, cordial, decorous, diplomatic, hospitable, magnanimous, tactful.

Fulsome means *excessive, especially regarding flattery.* Synonyms: adulatory, cloying, fawning, ingratiating, obsequious, profuse, saccharine, simpering, smarmy, sycophantic, toady, treacly, unctuous.

Tyrannical means *oppressive and controlling.* Synonyms: authoritarian, despotic, dictatorial, draconian, fascist, illiberal, imperious, totalitarian.

Martinet means *strict disciplinarian.* Synonyms: doctrinaire, dogmatist, pedant, stickler.

Group 86

Here's an excerpt from a movie. See if you can name the movie, describe the scene, and define the boldface vocabulary words. Check your answers on the following page.

LT. ARCHIE HICOX: . . . not exactly the **loquacious** type, is he?

LT. ALDO RAINE: Is that the kind of man you need, the loquacious type?

LT. ARCHIE HICOX: Fair point, Lieutenant.

LT. ALDO RAINE: Say you all get in trouble in there, what are we supposed to do, make bets on how it all comes out?

LT. ARCHIE HICOX: If we get into trouble, we can handle it. But if trouble does happen, we need you to make damn sure no Germans, or French, for that matter, escape from that basement. If Frau von Hammersmark's cover is compromised, the mission is **kaput.**

SGT. DONNY DONOWITZ: Speaking of Frau von Hammersmark, whose idea was it for the death trap **rendezvous?**

LT. ARCHIE HICOX: She chose the spot.

SGT. DONNY DONOWITZ: Oh, isn't that just dandy.

LT. ARCHIE HICOX: Look, she's not a military strategist. She's just an actress.

LT. ALDO RAINE: Well, you don't got to be Stonewall Jackson to know you don't want to fight in a basement.

Movie: _____

Scene: _____

Loquacious might mean _____

Kaput might mean _____

Rendezvous might mean _____

Hint: "That I cannot **abide.**"

Solutions

Let's see how you did. Check your answers and write the exact definitions. To help you memorize the vocabulary words, reread the movie excerpt or even act out the scene with a friend.

Movie: *Inglourious Basterds,* The Weinstein Company, 2009

Scene: This scene occurs right before the meet-up with Frau von Hammersmark in the tavern. Hicox prepares Stiglitz to remain calm if things go wrong and comments to Raine (Brad Pitt) about how quiet Stiglitz is. I love Donny Donowitz's Boston accent in this scene. He sounds like Click and Clack from the NPR weekly radio show *Car Talk.*

Inside Scoop: With a fun *allusion* (reference) to his movie *Fight Club,* Brad Pitt's character is upset that the meet-up is planned in a basement and states, "You know, fightin' in a basement offers a lot of difficulties."

Vocabulary in the Hint: Aldo Raine is famous for saying "That I cannot abide" with his thick Tennessee accent. *Abide* in this case means *tolerate.* It can also mean *obey.*

Loquacious means *talkative.* Synonyms: effusive, expansive, garrulous, prolix, verbose, voluble. Antonyms: reticent, taciturn. *Loqu-* implies *speaking,* as in *eloquent* (well-spoken), *grandiloquent* (using pompous, fancy language), and *colloquial* (informal speaking). *Grandiloquent* is a fancy, high-level vocab word that's easy to remember. It translates as *grand speaking,* a pretty good hint for *using pompous, fancy language.*

Kaput means *useless.*

Rendezvous means *meet up* and translates directly from French as "present yourselves."

Group 87

Here are two excerpts from a movie. See if you can name the movie, describe the scenes, and define the boldface vocabulary words. Check your answers on the following page.

DALE: Well, do you remember where he lives?

SAUL: Yeah, I know where he lives. What are you **insinuating,** like I'm forgetful?

DALE: *Insinuating,* good word.

SAUL: Oh, do you know what that means?

DALE: I do know what it means, believe it or not.

SAUL: (it means) *to seem like.*

———————

DALE: How could he know where you are?

SAUL: Um, heat-seeking missiles, um, bloodhounds and foxes . . . barracudas, . . .

DALE: I'm just . . . I'm kind of **flabbergasted** when you say things like that. It's weird.

SAUL: Thank you.

DALE: Not a compliment.

Movie: _____

Scenes: _____

_____

Insinuating might mean _____

Flabbergasted might mean _____

Hint: "In case you haven't noticed, which you haven't, 'cause from what I can tell, you don't notice anything, ever, we are not very functional when we're high."

Solutions

Let's see how you did. Check your answers and write the exact definitions. To help you memorize the vocabulary words, reread the movie excerpts or even act out the scenes with a friend.

Movie: *Pineapple Express,* Columbia Pictures, 2008

Scenes: In the first excerpt, Dale (Seth Rogen) and Saul (James Franco) are in Dale's car after a night of hiding out in the woods. They are discussing how to contact Red (they can't call him because they destroyed their phones to avoid being tracked down). In the next scene, they find Red (Danny McBride) and get into a bit of a scuffle. These guys are hilarious, and I love when Red quotes *Gladiator* during the fight: "What we do in life echoes in eternity." In the second excerpt, Saul offers his brainstorm of how Ted might find them.

Inside Scoop: Did you recognize Ken Jeong as one of the Asian drug lords? He was none other than Mr. Leslie Chow, the naked guy who jumps out of the trunk in *The Hangover!* He was also a doctor in *Knocked Up* and King of the LARPers in *Role Models!*

Insinuating means *implying*. I'm going to have to disagree with Saul on this one. *Insinuating* does not mean *to seem like,* though I think I can see where he was coming from with that definition. Synonym: intimating.

Flabbergasted means *astonished*. This excerpt was in the movie's trailer and is one of the most definitive exchanges in the film. Synonyms: boggled, confounded, dumbfounded, staggered, stupefied.

Group 88

Here are two excerpts from a movie. See if you can name the movie, describe the scenes, and define the boldface vocabulary words. Check your answers on the following page.

KELLER: And you didn't think that the United States military might need to know that you're keeping a **hostile** alien robot frozen in the basement?

BANACHEK: Until these events we had no **credible** threats to national security.

KELLER: Well, you got one now!

―――――――――

SAM WITWICKY: Megatron (that's what *they* call him), who's pretty much the **harbinger** of death, wants to use the cube to transform human technology to take over the universe. That's their plan.

Movie: _____

Scenes: _____

_____

Hostile might mean _____

_____

Credible might mean _____

_____

Harbinger might mean _____

_____

Hint: "The boy's **pheromone** levels suggest he wants to mate with the female."

Solutions

Let's see how you did. Check your answers and write the exact definitions. To help you memorize the vocabulary words, reread the movie excerpts or even act out the scenes with a friend.

Movie: *Transformers*, Paramount Pictures, 2007

Scenes: In the first excerpt, Keller (Jon Voight) has just been introduced to Sector 7 and the frozen Megatron (leader of the Decepticons) at the Hoover Dam. In the second excerpt, Sam is explaining what he knows to Keller.

Vocabulary in the Hint: *Pheromone* refers to *chemicals that animals secrete to affect other animals of their species.* Ratchet (medic of the Autobots) is, of course, referring, in this case, to sex pheromones, which communicate the desire to mate, and Sam (Shia LaBeouf) and Mikaela's (Megan Fox) embarrassed reactions to Ratchet's observation are hilarious!

Hostile means *unfriendly* or even *harmful*. In this case, for Megatron, who wants to destroy humans and dominate Earth, *harmful* is an understatement. *Bellicose* (warlike), *belligerent* (hostile and aggressive), *pugnacious* (eager to fight), or *truculent* (eager to fight) would be more appropriate.

Credible means *believable*. *Cred-* means *believe*, which helps you remember words like *creed* (beliefs), *incredulous* (disbelieving), and *credence* (believability). Synonyms: feasible, plausible, tenable.

Harbinger means *something that signals the approach of something else.* In *So I Married an Axe Murderer*, Charlie's (Mike Myers) girlfriend, who works in a Scottish butcher shop and serves up oodles of tasty haggis, is the "harbinger of haggis" (Group 79), and Megatron is the "harbinger of death." Synonyms: augury, forerunner, foretoken, forewarning, herald, indication, omen, portent, precursor, presage.

Group 89

Here's an excerpt from a movie. See if you can name the movie, describe the scene, and define the boldface vocabulary word. Check your answers on the following page.

RAY EMBREY: So you've used the door, the building's still **intact,** people are happy that you've arrived, they feel safe now, there's an officer there, and he's done a good job, so you might want to tell him he's done a good job.

JOHN: What the hell did I have to come for, Ray, if he's done a good job?

Movie: _____

Scene: _____

_____

Intact might mean _____

_____

Hint: "Your landing is your first impression. It's your superhero handshake. Don't come in too hot, OK, don't come in too boozy, and don't land on a $100,000 Mercedes. All right? People have to be happy that you've arrived."

Solutions

Let's see how you did. Check your answers and write the exact definition. To help you memorize the vocabulary word, reread the movie excerpt or even act out the scene with a friend.

Movie: *Hancock,* Columbia Pictures, 2008

Scene: John Hancock (Will Smith) saved Ray's life, so now Ray (Jason Bateman), a public relations consultant, is helping Hancock turn his image around so that people will respect and thank, rather than hate and berate, him. This movie is genius, a totally original superhero movie—gritty, but with true emotional appeal.

Intact means *complete* or *undamaged*. *Intact* actually breaks down to *in-,* meaning *not,* and *tact-,* which refers to *touch*. So *intact* means *not touched,* as in Hancock flew through a building thereby leaving it in ruins, but he missed the outhouse and left it **intact** (untouched, complete, undamaged). The word part *tact-* helps you remember **touch** words like *tactile,* which means *relating to the sense of **touch***.

Group 90

Here's an excerpt from a movie. See if you can name the movie, describe the scene, and define the boldface vocabulary word. Check your answers on the following page.

OFFICER MICHAELS: (*Watching a security tape of Fogel being punched during the liquor-store robbery.*) Your legs lifted off the ground.

OFFICER SLATER: Oh my God, that is **bona fide** . . . , man! Oh, you gotta keep that tape . . .

FOGEL: Well, don't you guys need it for evidence?

OFFICER MICHAELS: The only thing that's evidence of is that you can take a hit like a champ, man. Seriously.

Movie: _____

Scene: _____

_____

Bona fide might mean _____

_____

Hint: "I just want to go to the rooftops and scream 'I love my best friend, Evan!'"

Solutions

Let's see how you did. Check your answers and write the exact definition. To help you memorize the vocabulary word, reread the movie excerpt or even act out the scene with a friend.

Movie: *Superbad,* Columbia Pictures, 2007

Scene: Officer Slater (Bill Hader), Officer Michaels (Seth Rogen), and Fogel (Christopher Mintz-Plasse) are watching the security tape from the liquor-store robbery. In the tape, the robber punches Fogel.

Bonus *Superbad* Vocabulary: There are two lines from the *Superbad* screenplay that contain excellent standardized-test vocabulary that did not make the final cut of the film. Outside of the grocery store where Fogel works, he and Evan (Michael Cera) are talking about rooming together in college. Fogel tells Evan that he has three lava lamps and one strobe light. In the script, Evan responds, "We can't have three lava lamps. How **cliché** can you be?" *Cliché* is a great standardized-test vocabulary word that means *corny and overused.* Standardized tests also love the related words *banal* (overused and boring), and *hackneyed, platitudinous,* and *trite,* which mean *overused.* Lava lamps are the most stereotypic dorm-room accessory, so three of them might be a bit overdone, but I'm still with Fogel: three lava lamps and a strobe would make for a pretty groovy looking dorm room.

The second screenplay vocabulary word that was omitted from the movie is from the scene when Evan and Seth (Jonah Hill) wake up the morning after they had declared their love for each other (in the hint). They are uncomfortable and make small talk, and Seth says, "This is a really good pillow. **Ergonomic.**" *Ergonomic* means *well designed to provide comfort and safety* and is based on *erg* which is a *unit of work.* Seth's **ergonomic** pillow provides comfort from little work, that is, he would not have to shift around a lot to get comfortable. But, really he's just making conversation to hide his discomfort after the previous night's *bromance* (feelings of love between two heterosexual males).

Bona fide means *genuine.* Synonyms: authentic, indubitable, legitimate, veritable. Antonym: bogus (fake).

Quiz 9

I. Let's review some of the words that you've seen in Groups 81–90. Match each of the following words to the correct definition or synonym on the right. If you need help, refer back to the movie excerpts and definitions. Then check the solutions on page 234.

1. Mandate		A. Ruminative
2. Viscosity		B. Politic
3. Impetuous		C. Pertinacity
4. Sully		D. Fiat
5. Pensive		E. Rash
6. Judicious		F. Doctrinaire
7. Fortitude		G. Plausible
8. Implacable		H. Undamaged
9. Fulsome		I. Garrulous
10. Martinet		J. Gooeyness
11. Loquacious		K. Defile
12. Credible		L. Legitimate
13. Intact		M. Simpering
14. Bona fide		N. Platitudinous
15. Trite		O. Unappeasable

II. Let's review several of the word parts that you've seen in Groups 81–90. Match each of the following word parts to the correct definition or synonym on the right. Then check the solutions on page 234.

16. Im- (as in *implacable*)		A. Speaking
17. Loqu- (as in *loquacious*)		B. Feeling
18. Cred- (as in *credible*)		C. Write
19. Tact- (as in *tactile*)		D. Touch
Review from earlier groups:		E. Believe
20. -path (as in *apathy*)		F. Not
21. -scribe (as in *circumscribe*)		

Quiz 9 (continued)

III. Match each group of synonyms to its general meaning. Then check the solutions on page 234.

22. Astute
    Canny
    Judicious
    Percipient
    Politic
    Prudent
    Sagacious
    Shrewd

    A. Courage and strength

23. Audacity
    Fortitude
    Grit
    Indefatigability
    Intrepidity
    Mettle
    Pertinacity
    Pluck
    Resolve
    Tenacity

    B. Hostile and aggressive

24. Adulatory
    Fawning
    Fulsome
    Ingratiating
    Obsequious
    Simpering
    Smarmy
    Sycophantic
    Toady
    Unctuous

    C. Excessive flattery

25. Bellicose
    Belligerent
    Pugnacious
    Truculent

    D. Sensible

Group 91

Here's an excerpt from a movie. See if you can name the movie, describe the scene, and define the boldface vocabulary words. Check your answers on the following page.

NARRATOR: In a time where to be different was to be condemned, and to be **condemned** was to die, one man chose to question his God. From Fox Searchlight, five-time Academy Award winner Kirk Lazarus and MTV Movie Award Best Kiss winner Tobey Maguire, winner of the Beijing Film Festival's **coveted** Crying Monkey award, *Satan's Alley.*

Movie: _____

Scene: _____

_____

Condemned might mean _____

_____

Coveted might mean _____

_____

Hint: Les Grossman (Tom Cruise) presses a button, the rap song "Get Back" by Ludacris starts playing, and Grossman begins one of the most hilarious dance scenes in movie history—he finishes the dance at the end of the movie.

Solutions

Let's see how you did. Check your answers and write the exact definitions. To help you memorize the vocabulary words, reread the movie excerpt or even act out the scene with a friend.

Movie: *Tropic Thunder,* Paramount Pictures, 2008

Scene: This is one of the fictitious "previews" introducing the characters at the beginning of *Tropic Thunder*. In this preview, a spoof of *Brokeback Mountain,* Kirk Lazarus (Robert Downey, Jr.) plays a monk who falls in love with another monk, Tobey Maguire.

Hint Recap: Les Grossman (Tom Cruise) wants Tugg Speedman's (Ben Stiller) agent Peck (Matthew McConaughey) to forget about Speedman and is trying to bribe him with money and an airplane. *Tropic Thunder* features the very excellent Robert Downey Jr., Jack Black, Ben Stiller, Jay Baruchel, Nick Nolte, and Bill Hader, but Tom Cruise stole this movie. You should re-watch his dance scene as Les Grossman at the end of the movie. I'd say it's funnier than *Napoleon Dynamite*'s dance to Jamiroquai's "Canned Heat," funnier than Jim's striptease in *American Pie,* and funnier even than Evan and Seth's dance during the opening credits of *Superbad.*

Condemned means *denounced* or *convicted*. It actually comes from the word *damned,* as in "You've seen a ship with black sails that's crewed by the **damned** and captained by a man so evil that Hell itself spat him back out?" (*Pirates of the Caribbean: The Curse of the Black Pearl*). Synonyms: berated, castigated, censured, chastised, inculpated, rebuked, reprimanded, reproved, reviled.

Coveted means *desired*.

Here's an excerpt from a movie. See if you can name the movie, describe the scene, and define the boldface vocabulary word. Check your answers on the following page.

LORD CUTLER BECKETT: I care not for cursed Aztec gold. My desires are not so **provincial.** There's more than one chest of value in these waters. So perhaps you may wish to enhance your offer.

Movie: _____

Scene: _____

_____

Provincial might mean _____

_____

Hint: Does he mean Davey Jones' treasure chest, or is he, ever so rudely, speaking of Keira Knightley's chest?

Solutions

Let's see how you did. Check your answers and write the exact definition. To help you memorize the vocabulary word, reread the movie excerpt or even act out the scene with a friend.

Movie: *Pirates of the Caribbean: Dead Man's Chest,* Walt Disney Pictures, 2006

Scene: Lord Beckett (Tom Hollander) has arrested Elizabeth (Keira Knightley) and Will Turner (Orlando Bloom) before their wedding and demands that they find Jack Sparrow (Johnny Depp). Beckett wants them to get Sparrow's compass and will *barter* (trade) Elizabeth and Will's pardons for the compass—this is a unique compass that points in the direction of whatever its possessor most truly wants.

Provincial means *narrow-minded* or *unsophisticated*. Beckett means that his desires are more **sophisticated** and involve more than simply seeking gold. Synonyms: insular, parochial.

Group 93

Here's an excerpt from a movie. See if you can name the movie, describe the scene, and define the boldface vocabulary words. Check your answers on the following page.

JAY: Now you're being **condescending**. See, you've been warned, a'ight. Let's move forward **amicably**.

CUSTOMER: OK. Well check this out though. First of all, you're throwing too many big words at me. OK now, because I don't understand them, I'm gonna take 'em as disrespect. Watch your mouth and help me with the sale.

Movie: _____

Scene: _____

_____

Condescending might mean _____

_____

Amicably might mean _____

_____

Hint: "We gonna need more wax!"

Solutions

Let's see how you did. Check your answers and write the exact definitions. To help you memorize the vocabulary words, reread the movie excerpt or even act out the scene with a friend.

Movie: *The 40-Year-Old Virgin,* Universal Pictures, 2005

Scene: After Andy (Steve Carell) is promoted to floor manager, Jay (Romany Malco) and a customer are arguing, and Paula (Jane Lynch), the manager, sends Andy over to handle it. Unless you've seen *40-Year-Old Virgin* quite a few times, this was probably a tough quote to identify, so I gave a very helpful hint, "We gonna need more wax!" I'd put the chest-waxing scene in the Funniest Movie Scenes of All Time, along with Owen Wilson and Vince Vaughn's improvised "lock it up" exchange in *Wedding Crashers;* Bill Murray's treadmill scene in *Lost in Translation;* the taser scene in *The Hangover;* Seth Rogen and James Franco's running in the dark scene after Franco's character panics in *Pineapple Express;* and (drum role) . . . Tom Cruise's dance to "Get Back" in *Tropic Thunder!*

Inside Scoop: To make the chest-waxing scene realistic, the actress playing the beautician is *actually* waxing Steve Carell's chest!

Condescending means *looking down on* or *treating as inferior*. Synonym: patronizing.

Amicably means *in a friendly way* and comes from the Latin word *amicus,* which means *friend,* like *amigo* in Spanish, or *ami* in French. Synonyms for *amicable:* affable, amiable, cordial, genial, simpatico. *Simpatico* sounds like a word that Andy would use in this movie. He'd say it in a weird way, and then there'd be an awkward silence.

Group 94

Here are two excerpts from a movie. See if you can name the movie, describe the scenes, and define the boldface vocabulary words. Check your answers on the following page.

CHRIS: Mr. Franz, I think careers are a twentieth-century invention and I don't want one. You don't need to worry about me. I have a college education. I'm not **destitute**. I'm living like this by choice.

———————

CHRIS: (*working on leather*) It's amazing how **malleable** this is.

MR. FRANZ: Yeah, it is.

CHRIS: When the leather is wet, you can really . . .

MR. FRANZ: It's like butter.

Movie: _____

Scenes: _____

_____

Destitute might mean _____

_____

Malleable might mean _____

_____

Hint: Zach Galifianakis (Alan of *The Hangover*) makes a cameo as Kevin, the guy who teaches Chris how to hunt for and preserve meat in the wild.

Solutions

Let's see how you did. Check your answers and write the exact definitions. To help you memorize the vocabulary words, reread the movie excerpts or even act out the scenes with a friend.

Movie: *Into the Wild,* Paramount Vantage, 2007

Scenes: Chris McCandless (Emile Hirsch) spends some time living with Mr. Franz (Hal Holbrook) before he heads to Alaska.

Destitute means *penniless* or *poverty-stricken*. Synonyms: impecunious, impoverished, indigent, insolvent, penurious. I remember the meaning of *penurious* (penniless or cheap) because it looks a lot like *penny*.

Malleable means *flexible* or *easily bent*. *Malleable* looks like *mallet-able,* which is not a coincidence, because *malleable* technically means *able to be bent or shaped with a **mallet** (hammer),* like in metalwork and leatherwork (which Chris and Mr. Franz are doing). Synonyms: compliant, ductile, pliable, tractable. Antonym: intractable.

Here's an excerpt from a movie. See if you can name the movie, describe the scene, and define the boldface vocabulary words. Check your answers on the following page.

COLONEL HANS LANDA: I understand your **trepidation** in repeating it. Heydrich apparently hates the **moniker** the good people of Prague have **bestowed** upon him . . . If a rat were to scamper through your front door, right now, would you greet it with **hostility**?

PERRIER LaPADITE: I suppose I would.

COLONEL HANS LANDA: Has the rat even done anything to you to create this **animosity** you feel toward him?

Movie: _____

Scene: _____

_____

Trepidation might mean _____

Moniker might mean _____

Bestowed might mean _____

Hostility might mean _____

Animosity might mean _____

Hint: "Now, y'all might've heard rumors about the **armada** happening soon. Well, we'll be leaving a little earlier. We're gonna be dropped into France, dressed as civilians."

Solutions

Let's see how you did. Check your answers and write the exact definitions. To help you memorize the vocabulary words, reread the movie excerpt or even act out the scene with a friend.

Movie: *Inglourious Basterds,* The Weinstein Company, 2009

Scene: This excerpt is from the opening scene when SS Colonel Landa (Christoph Waltz) is questioning Perrier LaPadite (Dennis Menochet), a milk farmer.

Vocabulary in the Hint: *Armada* means *fleet.* Synonym: flotilla. This quote is from Brad Pitt's character, Lieutenant Aldo Raine, who is giving an orientation to new members of the Inglourious Basterds. The word *inglorious* from the title of this film is also a high-level vocabulary word. *Inglorious* means *shameful* or *not famous.* You might remember hearing this word during a powerful scene in the film *300.* In front of the Spartan council, Theron (Dominic West) falsely accuses King Leonidas' wife, Queen Gorgo (Lena Headey), of bribing him and states, "What queen-like behavior. Remove her from this chamber before she infects us further with her **inglorious** and shabby self." (In fact, Queen Gorgo had not tried to bribe Theron, and Theron is the traitor, which Gorgo then proves to the Council.)

Trepidation means *fear.* Synonyms: apprehension, disquiet, foreboding.

Moniker means *nickname.* Synonyms: pseudonym, sobriquet.

Bestowed means *gave.* Synonyms: accorded, afforded, granted, vouchsafed.

Hostility means *unfriendliness* or *aggression.* Synonyms: acrimony, animosity, antagonism, antipathy, belligerence, enmity, malevolence, malice, rancor, truculence, venom.

Animosity means *strong hostility.* Synonyms: acrimony, antagonism, antipathy, belligerence, enmity, malevolence, malice, rancor, truculence, venom.

Group 96

Here's an excerpt from a movie. See if you can name the movie, describe the scene, and define the boldface vocabulary words. Check your answers on the following page.

RICKY BOBBY: Really, smarty pants? What did French land give us?

JEAN GIRARD: We invented **democracy, existentialism,** and the **ménage à trois.**

CAL: Those are three pretty good things.

Movie: _____

Scene: _____

_____

Democracy might mean _____

_____

Existentialism might mean _____

_____

Ménage à trois might mean _____

_____

Hint: "Shake 'n' bake!"

Solutions

Let's see how you did. Check your answers and write the exact definitions. To help you memorize the vocabulary words, reread the movie excerpt or even act out the scene with a friend.

Movie: *Talladega Nights: The Ballad of Ricky Bobby,* Columbia Pictures, 2006

Scene: In this excerpt, Ricky Bobby (Will Ferrell) and Cal (John C. Reilly) are hanging out at the Pitt Stop bar when suddenly the music changes to jazz and the guys freak out. Jean Girard emerges and introduces himself as the greatest driver in the world. Jean is French, so he and Ricky Bobby begin comparing what each country has given the world.

Inside Scoop: Did you recognize Sacha Baron Cohen, a.k.a. Borat, a.k.a. Ali G, a.k.a. Brüno, as Jean Girard?

Democracy means *government of the people, run by elected officials.* Demo- means *people,* as in *demographics* (the study of populations of people), and *-cracy* means *rule,* so *democracy* means *people rule—government by the people.* The suffix *-cracy* reminds me of *-archy* (ruler) along with *monarchy* (*mono-* means *one,* so *monarchy* means *rule by one*—usually by a king or queen), *oligarchy* (*oligo-* means *a small number,* so *oligarchy* means *rule by a small group of individuals*), *matriarchy* (rule by women), and *plutarchy* (rule by the wealthy), which you learned from *Ferris Bueller's Day Off* (Group 29).

Existentialism refers to the *philosophy that people must find their own meaning to existence.*

Ménage à trois literally translates from French as *household of three* and refers to *three people together in a sexual relationship.* This word will probably not show up on your SAT, but it can help you remember SAT words *ménage* (members of a **household**) and *menagerie* (collection of diverse people, animals, or things—like a **household** of wild animals, diverse people, or unusual things).

Group 97

Here's an excerpt from a movie. See if you can name the movie, describe the scene, and define the boldface vocabulary words. Check your answers on the following page.

Young Elizabeth: (*standing at the bow of a ship and singing*) Drink up me hearties, yo ho! We kidnap and ravage and don't give a hoot. Drink up me hearties, yo ho! Yo ho, yo ho, a pirate's life for me. We **extort**, we **pilfer**, we **filch** and **sack**. Drink up . . .

Gibbs: Quiet, missy! Cursed pirates sail these waters. You don't want to bring them down on us, now, do ya?

Norrington: Mr. Gibbs, that will do!

Gibbs: She was singing about pirates. Bad luck to be singing about pirates with us **mired** in this unnatural fog. Mark my words . . .

Young Elizabeth: I think it'd be rather exciting to meet a pirate.

Norrington: Think again, Miss Swann. **Vile** and **dissolute** creatures, the lot of them.

Movie: _____

Scene: _____

Extort might mean_____

Pilfer might mean _____

Filch might mean _____

Sack might mean _____

Mired might mean _____

Vile might mean _____

Dissolute might mean _____

Hint: Later in this film, Keira Knightley plays grown-up Elizabeth.

Solutions

Let's see how you did. Check your answers and write the exact definitions. To help you memorize the vocabulary words, reread the movie excerpt or even act out the scene with a friend.

Movie: *Pirates of the Caribbean: The Curse of the Black Pearl,* Walt Disney Pictures, 2003

Scene: Young Elizabeth is singing on the boat just before they fish young Will Turner from the sea. She says, "I think it'd be rather exciting to meet a pirate," and she gets her wish, several times over.

Extort, Pilfer, Filch, and Sack all mean *steal. Extort* implies **steal by force.** Now you know four words for *steal;* memorize Elizabeth's song and you'll never be at a loss for a synonym for *steal.*

Mired means *slowed down,* usually by mud. In fact, a *mire* is a **muddy swamp or bog.**

Vile means *very unpleasant* or *evil.* Interestingly, *vile* and *evil* have the exact same letters, but rearranged. That's called an *anagram,* like Hannibal Lecter's puzzles in the classic (and terrifying) movie *Silence of the Lambs.*

Dissolute means *immoral.* Synonyms: debauched, degenerate, depraved.

Group 98

Here's an excerpt from a movie. See if you can name the movie, describe the scene, and define the boldface vocabulary words. Check your answers on the following page.

You have many questions, and though the process has **altered** your consciousness, you remain **irrevocably** human. **Ergo,** some of my answers you will understand, and some of them you will not. **Concordantly,** while your first question may be the most **pertinent,** you may or may not realize it is also the most **irrelevant** . . . Your life is the sum of a remainder of an unbalanced equation **inherent** to the programming of the . . . You are the **eventuality** of an **anomaly,** which despite my sincerest efforts I have been unable to eliminate from what is otherwise a harmony of mathematical precision. While it remains a burden **assiduously** avoided, it is not unexpected, and thus not beyond a measure of control, which has led you, **inexorably,** here.

Movie: _____

Scene: _____

_____

Hint: "I'm trying to free your mind, Neo. But I can only show you the door. You're the one that has to walk through it."

Group 98 (continued)

Altered might mean _____

_____

Irrevocably might mean _____

_____

Ergo might mean _____

_____

Concordantly might mean _____

_____

Pertinent might mean _____

_____

Irrelevant might mean _____

_____

Inherent might mean _____

_____

Eventuality might mean _____

_____

Anomaly might mean _____

_____

Assiduously might mean _____

_____

Inexorably might mean _____

_____

Solutions

Let's see how you did. Check your answers and write the exact definitions. To help you memorize the vocabulary words, reread the movie excerpt or even act out the scene with a friend.

Movie: *The Matrix: Reloaded,* Warner Bros., 2003

Scene: This is the Architect's conversation with Neo (Keanu Reeves) in that groovy chamber with all the TVs, after Neo has tracked him down. I remember hearing this monologue in the theater and thinking, "What the pickle did you just say?" I'm not sure who uses bigger words, *The Matrix*'s Architect or V from *V for Vendetta*.

Solutions (continued)

Altered means *changed*. Synonym: permuted.

Irrevocably means *permanently*. Synonym: immutably.

Ergo means *therefore*. Synonyms: consequently, hence, whence.

Concordantly means *similarly*.

Pertinent means *relevant*. Synonyms: apposite, apropos, germane.

Irrelevant means *unimportant*. Synonyms: immaterial, inapposite.

Inherent means *natural* or *inborn*. Synonyms: innate, intrinsic.

Eventuality means *possibility*. You learned this word from *Casino Royale*'s Vesper Lynd (Group 51) as a synonym for *contingency*.

Anomaly means *glitch* or *irregularity*. Synonyms: aberration, incongruity.

Assiduously means *diligently*. Synonyms: conscientiously, meticulously, punctiliously, sedulously.

Inexorably means *unavoidably*. Synonyms: implacably, inevitably, interminably, intransigently, irrevocably, relentlessly, unceasingly, unrelentingly, unremittingly.

Group 99

Here's an excerpt from a movie. See if you can name the movie, describe the scene, and define the boldface vocabulary words. Check your answers on the following page.

JOHN KEATING: Have you ever told your father what you just told me? About your passion for acting? You ever show him that?

NEIL PERRY: I can't.

JOHN KEATING: Why not?

NEIL PERRY: I can't talk to him this way.

JOHN KEATING: Then you're acting for him, too. You're playing the part of the **dutiful** son. Now, I know this sounds impossible, but you have to talk to him. You have to show him who you are, what your heart is!

NEIL PERRY: I know what he'll say! He'll tell me that acting's a **whim** and I should forget it, "they're counting on me." He'll just tell me to put it out of my mind for my own good.

JOHN KEATING: You are not an **indentured** servant! It's not a whim for you; you prove it to him by your **conviction** and your passion! You show him that, and if he still doesn't believe you, well, by then, you'll be out of school and can do anything you want.

Movie: _____

Scene: _____

Dutiful might mean _____

Whim might mean _____

Indentured might mean _____

Conviction might mean _____

Hint: "Carpe diem. Seize the day, boys. Make your lives extraordinary!"

Solutions

Let's see how you did. Check your answers and write the exact definitions. To help you memorize the vocabulary words, reread the movie excerpt or even act out the scene with a friend.

Movie: *Dead Poets Society,* Touchstone Pictures, 1989

Scene: Neil (Robert Sean Leonard) wants to act in *A Midsummer Night's Dream*, but his dad forbids it. He is asking for advice from his teacher, Mr. Keating (Robin Williams).

Dutiful means *fulfilling a duty or obligation.* You can see this from the context: by giving up acting, Neil believes that he would be **fulfilling the obligations** placed on him by his father. Synonyms: acquiescent, amenable, biddable, compliant, deferential, malleable, obedient, obsequious, pliable, pliant, servile, submissive, subservient, tractable. Antonym: disobedient.

Whim means *sudden urge.* Synonyms: caprice, fickleness, foible, megrim, vagary. Standardized tests also love to use the synonyms for *whimsical* (acting on urges): capricious, erratic, fickle, inconstant, mercurial, mutable, protean, volatile.

Indentured means *indebted* or *bound.* You probably learned about **indentured** servants in U.S. History class, but you can also remember the meaning of this word just by thinking of your grandfather's **dentures,** which **bind** his "false teeth" to his gums.

Conviction means *sureness* and comes from the word *convince;* when you have *conviction,* you are totally *convinced—you're sure.* Of course, it can also refer to *a jury's pronouncement of guilt.* Synonym: certitude.

Group  100

Here's an excerpt from a movie. See if you can name the movie, describe the scene, and define the boldface vocabulary words. Check your answers on the following page.

░░░░░░░░░░░░░░░░░░░░░░░░░░░░░░░░░░░

(*Mr. Keaton and Mr. McManus are holding Kobayashi at gunpoint.*)

KOBAYASHI: I **implore** you, Mr. Keaton, believe me, Mr. Söze is very real and very determined.

KEATON: We'll see.

KOBAYASHI: Before you . . . do me in, Mr. McManus, you will let me finish my business with Ms. Finneran first, won't you?

KEATON: What did you say?

KOBAYASHI: Edie Finneran. She's upstairs in my office for an **extradition deposition.** I requested she be put on the case personally. She flew in yesterday. No matter. Kill away, Mr. McManus.

░░░░░░░░░░░░░░░░░░░░░░░░░░░░░░░░░░░

Movie: _____

Scene: _____

_____

Implore might mean _____

_____

Extradition might mean _____

_____

Deposition might mean _____

_____

Hint: "Keyser Söze!"

Solutions

Let's see how you did. Check your answers and write the exact definitions. To help you memorize the vocabulary words, reread the movie excerpt or even act out the scene with a friend.

Movie: *The Usual Suspects,* Gramercy Pictures, 1995

Scene: Kobayashi (Pete Postlethwaite), on behalf of Keyser Söze, is *blackmailing* (forcing through threats) known criminals Mr. Keaton (Gabriel Byrne) and Mr. McManus (Stephen Baldwin) to *thwart* (prevent) a drug deal that will occur on a ship in the harbor of San Pedro, California. In the excerpt, Mr. Keaton and Mr. McManus threaten Kobayashi's life if he will not call off the deal, but he trumps them by mentioning that he has Keaton's girlfriend, Edie Finneran. Did you get the Keyser Söze hint? He's the ultra bad guy pulling the strings. I'd say that this movie is tied with *The Sixth Sense* for best surprise ending. Do you remember it?

Implore means *beg.* Synonyms: beseech, entreat, importune.

Extradition means *moving of a criminal or criminal suspect from one country to another.* You learned this word in the definition of *rendition* from *The Bourne Ultimatum* (Group 67). *Rendition* in that case meant *covert extradition* (secretly moving a criminal or criminal suspect from one country to another). Synonyms: deportation, repatriation.

Deposition means *the official statement of a witness taken outside of the courtroom.* Synonym: affidavit. So an ***extradition deposition*** means that Kobayashi is recording Edie's **official statement** about someone being **deported.**

Quiz 10

I. Let's review some of the words that you've seen in Groups 91–100. Match each of the following words to the correct definition or synonym on the right. If you need help, refer back to the movie excerpts and definitions. Then check the solutions on page 234.

1. Condemn
2. Provincial
3. Amicable
4. Destitute
5. Malleable
6. Trepidation
7. Animosity
8. Extort
9. Dissolute
10. Anomaly
11. Assiduously
12. Inexorably
13. Conviction
14. Whim
15. Implore

A. Genial
B. Disquiet
C. Steal
D. Castigate
E. Sedulously
F. Tractable
G. Certitude
H. Parochial
I. Indigent
J. Entreat
K. Caprice
L. Unrelentingly
M. Acrimony
N. Aberration
O. Debauched

II. Let's review several of the word parts that you've seen in Groups 91–100. Match each of the following word parts to the correct definition or synonym on the right. Then check the solutions on page 234.

16. Demo- (as in *democracy*)
17. -cracy (as in *bureaucracy*)
18. Mono- (as in *monarchy*)
Review from earlier groups:
19. Tact- (as in *tactile*)
20. Loqu- (as in *loquacious*)
21. Trans- (as in *transcription*)

A. One
B. Speak
C. Rule
D. People
E. Across
F. Touch

Quiz 10 (continued)

III. Match each group of synonyms to its general meaning. Then check the solutions on page 234.

22. Affable
    Amiable
    Amicable
    Genial
    Simpatico

A. Diligently

23. Acrimony
    Animosity
    Antipathy
    Belligerence
    Enmity
    Malevolence
    Malice
    Rancor
    Truculence
    Venom

B. Friendly

24. Inherent
    Innate
    Intrinsic

C. Beg

25. Assiduously
    Meticulously
    Punctiliously
    Sedulously

D. Hostility

26. Caprice
    Megrim
    Vagary

E. Sudden urge

27. Beseech
    Entreat
    Implore
    Importune

F. Inborn

Quiz Solutions

Quiz 1	Quiz 2	Quiz 3	Quiz 4	Quiz 5
1. I	1. H	1. F	1. F	1. K
2. F	2. F	2. J	2. A	2. F
3. A	3. A	3. A	3. H	3. E
4. E	4. G	4. G	4. B	4. O
5. B	5. B	5. B	5. K	5. A
6. J	6. L	6. K	6. C	6. J
7. C	7. I	7. O	7. D	7. B
8. D	8. J	8. C	8. M	8. M
9. G	9. K	9. N	9. O	9. D
10. M	10. C	10. D	10. E	10. G
11. L	11. D	11. E	11. L	11. R
12. H	12. E	12. M	12. N	12. T
13. O	13. O	13. H	13. I	13. S
14. K	14. N	14. L	14. J	14. C
15. N	15. M	15. I	15. G	15. Q
16. E	16. C or F	16. D	16. D	16. I
17. D	17. C or F	17. C or E	17. E	17. L
18. B	18. D	18. C or E	18. F	18. H
19. A	19. B	19. A	19. B	19. N
20. F	20. A	20. F	20. A	20. P
21. C	21. E	21. B	21. C	21. B
22. E	22. D	22. E	22. C	22. A
23. D	23. F	23. A	23. E	23. D
24. A	24. A	24. D	24. A	24. C
25. F	25. C	25. B	25. B	25. E
26. C	26. B	26. C	26. D	26. A
27. B	27. E			27. B

Quiz Solutions (continued)

Quiz 6	Quiz 7	Quiz 8	Quiz 9	Quiz 10
1. E	1. E	1. D	1. D	1. D
2. A	2. H	2. H	2. J	2. H
3. L	3. G	3. A	3. E	3. A
4. G	4. A	4. M	4. K	4. I
5. B	5. C	5. B	5. A	5. F
6. K	6. I	6. J	6. B	6. B
7. C	7. D	7. L	7. C	7. M
8. N	8. L	8. O	8. O	8. C
9. D	9. O	9. N	9. M	9. O
10. O	10. N	10. K	10. F	10. N
11. M	11. B	11. C	11. I	11. E
12. F	12. M	12. F	12. G	12. L
13. H	13. K	13. E	13. H	13. G
14. J	14. J	14. G	14. L	14. K
15. I	15. F	15. I	15. N	15. J
16. B	16. C	16. E	16. F	16. D
17. E	17. F	17. A	17. A	17. C
18. F	18. A	18. F	18. E	18. A
19. A	19. E	19. B	19. D	19. F
20. C	20. B	20. D	20. B	20. B
21. D	21. D	21. C	21. C	21. E
22. C	22. E	22. F	22. D	22. B
23. F	23. D	23. C	23. A	23. D
24. A	24. F	24. E	24. C	24. F
25. B	25. C	25. A	25. B	25. A
26. E	26. A	26. D		26. E
27. D	27. B	27. B		27. C

Glossary

Aberration abnormality, a person who behaves in an unacceptable and abnormal way. Synonyms: *anomaly, deviation, divergence, perversion*

Abides obeys, tolerates

Absolute total, complete. Synonyms: *categorical, consummate, unconditional, unmitigated, unqualified*

Abstract conceptual

Abstraction ideas or theories

Absurd unreasonable or ridiculous. Synonyms: *farcical, inane, ludicrous, preposterous, risible*

Accolades honors. Synonyms: *kudos, plaudits*

Accrue accumulate or amass

Acute sharp, smart, or severe. Synonyms: *astute, canny, incisive, judicious, keen, perspicacious, sagacious, savvy, shrewd, wise*

Affable friendly and easy to hang out with. Synonyms: *amiable, amicable, cordial, genial, gregarious, simpatico*

Alloy mixture. Synonyms: *amalgam, composite, fusion*

Allusion reference

Altered changed. Synonym: *permuted*

Ambiguous unclear, open to more than one interpretation

Ambivalent having mixed feelings

Amicably in a friendly way. Synonyms for amicable: *affable, amiable, cordial, genial, simpatico*

Amorphous without a clear form or shape. Synonyms: *nebulous, vague*

Anarchists people who believe in total individual freedom and the absence of law

Anarcho-syndicalist a system of government self-managed by workers

Anarchy disorder or the absence of law. Synonyms: *bedlam, chaos, mayhem, pandemonium, turmoil*

Animosity strong hatred or hostility. Synonyms: *acrimony, antagonism, antipathy, belligerence, enmity, malevolence, malice, rancor, truculence, venom*

Anointed appointed to a powerful or important position

Anomaly irregularity or abnormality. Synonyms: *aberration, incongruity*

Antiquity the ancient past

Apartheid policy of segregation based on race

Apathy lack of interest. Synonyms: *dispassion, ennui, indifference, insouciance*

Apocalypse total destruction. Synonyms: *calamity, cataclysm, catastrophe*

Apogee highest point. Synonyms: *acme, apex, climax, peak, pinnacle, zenith*. Antonyms: *nadir, perigee*

Apt appropriate, likely, or able. Synonyms: *apposite, apropos, germane, pertinent*

Aptitude talent. Synonym: *faculty*

Arduous difficult and requiring hard work. Synonyms: *Herculean, laborious, onerous, toilsome*

Armada fleet. Synonym: *flotilla*

Articulate able to express ideas clearly. Synonym: *eloquent*

Articulated communicated

Artifice trickery

Artificial fake, human-made rather than naturally occurring. Synonyms: *bogus, contrived, ersatz, fabricated, faux, feigned, inorganic, mock, spurious, synthetic*

Asset resource

Assiduously diligently. Synonyms: *conscientiously, meticulously, punctiliously, sedulously*

Astute intelligent and insightful. Synonyms: *canny, incisive, judicious, keen, perspicacious, sagacious, savvy, shrewd, wise*

Audible hearable, change of plans (in football)

Audition hearing

Aural relating to the ear

Autocracy government ruled by one individual with complete power. Synonym: *dictatorship*

Autonomous self-governing. Synonyms: *independent, sovereign*

Axiom accepted truth. Synonyms: *adage, aphorism, apothegm, dictum, gnome, maxim, principle, truism*

Balks hesitates

Banal overused and boring

Barren empty, bleak, or lifeless. Synonyms: *desolate, infecund, infertile, sterile*

Bellicose aggressive or warlike. Synonyms: *antagonistic, belligerent, contentious, hawkish, inimical, pugnacious, truculent*

Belligerent hostile and aggressive. Synonyms: *bellicose, inimical, pugnacious, truculent*

Bemused confused. Synonyms: *bewildered, flummoxed, nonplussed*

Benign king or harmless. Synonyms: *innocuous, nonmalignant*

Bereft of lacking. Synonym: *sans*

Beset troubled or afflicted. Synonyms: *assailed, bedeviled, beleaguered, besieged, harassed, inundated, oppressed, plagued, tormented*

Bestowed gave. Synonyms: *accorded, afforded, granted, vouchsafed*

Bevy large group. Synonyms: *horde, throng*

Bona fide genuine. Synonyms: *authentic, indubitable, legitimate, veritable.* Antonym: *bogus (fake)*

Boulangerie bakery (in French)

Brawn physical strength

Breadth width

Brevity briefness. Antonym: *verbosity*

Brute crude or violent

Bureaucracy the officials and administrative procedures of a government

Bureaucratic using excessively complicated rules of procedure

Callous insensitive

Cameos small roles

Candid unrehearsed, honest

Capricious unpredictable or changing too easily. Synonyms: *erratic, fickle, mercurial*

Catastrophic disastrous. Synonyms: *apocalyptic, calamitous, cataclysmic*

Categorically absolutely or explicitly. Synonyms: *unequivocally, unqualifiedly*

Chaos disorder. Synonyms: *anarchy, bedlam, mayhem, pandemonium, turmoil*

Charity kindness; giving help or money to those in need. Synonyms: *altruism, amity, beneficence, benevolence, caritas, compassion, goodwill, humanity, mercy, munificence, philanthropy, tolerance*

Cipher code. Synonym: *cryptogram*

Circumscribe write around something, confine and restrict

Circumstantial indirect

Clairvoyance psychic powers, often used to predict the future. Synonym: *prescience*

Cliché overused

Codicil addition, like an amendment to the U.S. constitution. Synonyms: *amendment, appendix, corollary*

Colloquial informal speaking

Comely attractive. Synonyms: *beauteous, fair, fetching, prepossessing, pulchritudinous*

Commencing beginning

Compensate pay back or make up for. Synonyms: *atone, expiate, indemnify, make amends, make reparation, recompense, rectify, remunerate, requite*

Compromised endangered, weakened, or made concessions to arrive at an agreement. Synonym: *jeopardized*

Concise lots of information cut down to what's most important. Synonym: *succinct*

Concordantly similarly

Condemned denounced or convicted. Synonyms: *berated, castigated, censured, chastised, inculpated, rebuked, reprimanded, reproached, reproved, reviled*

Condescending looking down on or treating as inferior. Synonym: *patronizing*

Condone reluctantly accept or approve. Synonym: *sanction*

Conjure materialize or summon

Console comfort. Synonym: *solace*

Conspirator a person who makes secret plans with another

Constructs theories, usually created without much solid evidence

Contingency possibility. Synonym: *eventuality*

Conventional traditional or ordinary

Conviction sureness, a jury's pronouncement of guilt. Synonym: *certitude*

Copious plentiful. Synonyms: *abundant, bountiful, profuse, prolific.* Antonym: *sparse*

Corollary offshoot or consequence

Cortex the outer layer of the front part of the brain

Cougars slang word for older women who seek out younger men

Countermanded reversed, cancelled, or stopped. Synonyms: *abrogated, annulled, nullified, quashed, repealed, rescinded, revoked, voided*

Covert hidden or secret. Synonyms: *clandestine, furtive, surreptitious.* Antonym: *obvious*

Coveted desired

Credence believability

Credible believable. Synonyms: *feasible, plausible, tenable*

Creed set of beliefs. Synonyms: *canon, doctrine, dogma, ideology, precepts, tenets*

Crude simple, vulgar, or unrefined

Cynical distrusting the motives of others. Synonyms: *dubious, skeptical*

Decadence excessive self-indulgence. Synonyms: *debauchery, degeneracy, depravity, hedonism, immoderateness, intemperance, licentiousness, vice*

Deduce conclude by logic

Demise destruction or death. Synonyms: *expiry, quietus*

Democracy government of the people, run by elected officials

Demographics the study of populations of people

Deposition the official statement of a witness taken outside of the courtroom. Synonym: *affidavit*

Depravity immorality. Synonyms: *corruption, debauchery, degeneracy, deviance, dissipation, indecency, iniquity, lechery, licentiousness, obscenity, perversion, profligacy, prurience, turpitude, vice*

Derogatory disrespectfully critical. Synonyms: *defamatory, denigrating, deprecating, depreciatory, disparaging, pejorative*

Descendants relatives that come after. Antonym: *ancestors*

Desperate distressed, hopeless, or needy. Synonyms: *desolate, forlorn*

Destitute penniless or poverty-stricken. Synonyms: *impecunious, impoverished, indigent, insolvent, penurious*

Dictatorship government ruled by one individual with complete power. Synonym: *autocracy*

Diffusionism the theory that similarities between cultures have been spread from one culture to another

Discreet inconspicuous, tactful (sensitive in dealing with others). Synonyms: *chary, circumspect, prudent, understated, unobtrusive*

Dispirited depressed

Disposition personality or character. Synonyms: *constitution, temperament*

Dissolute immoral. Synonyms: *debauched, degenerate, depraved*

Divination predicting the future with supernatural means

Divine discover or predict; pertaining to God, noble, admirable

Docile unquestioningly obedient. Synonyms: *acquiescent, amenable, biddable, compliant, deferential, malleable, pliant, submissive, unassertive*

Dogma system of beliefs presented as indisputable. Synonyms: *canon, creed, doctrine, precept, tenet*

Double entendre double meaning

Dovetailing fitting together easily

Dross trash. Synonyms: *chaff, debris, detritus, dreck, flotsam*

Dutiful fulfilling a duty or obligation. Synonyms: *acquiescent, amenable, biddable, compliant, deferential, malleable, obedient, obsequious, pliable, pliant, servile, submissive, subservient, tractable.* Antonym: *disobedient*

Dynamic changing, energetic, or bold

Eccentric an unconventional or odd person. Synonyms: *idiosyncratic, nonconformist*

Echelon level

Effusive gushing, unrestrained speaking or writing. Synonyms: *expansive, garrulous, loquacious, prolix, verbose, voluble.* Antonyms: *restrained, reticent, taciturn*

Egalitarian the belief that all people are equal and deserve equal rights. Synonym: *democratic*

Egregious shockingly bad. Synonyms: *abhorrent, abominable, appalling, atrocious, dire, grievous, heinous, intolerable*

Elemental representing the power of nature; essential or basic

Elite cream of the crop, the best. Synonym: *nonpareil*

Eloquent well-spoken

Emancipated freed

Empirical observed or experienced, rather than theorized. Synonym: *heuristic*

Encrypted coded to keep secret. Synonym: *ciphered*

Endowed equipped or blessed

Enhanced increased or improved

Ensnared caught or trapped. Synonyms: *embroiled, enmeshed, entangled*

Epilogue conclusion

Epiphany sudden realization of great truth. Synonym: *revelation*

Era time period of history. Synonyms: *eon, epoch*

Eradicate destroy completely. Synonyms: *annihilate, expunge, obliterate*

Erg a unit of work

Ergo therefore. Synonyms: *consequently, hence, whence*

Ergonomic well designed to provide comfort

Erroneous incorrect. Synonyms: *fallacious, specious*

Escort one who accompanies

Etiquette proper or polite behavior. Synonyms: *decorum, propriety, protocol*

Eulogize praise, often in a speech at a funeral. Synonym: *extol.* Antonym: *censure (criticize severely)*

Eulogy written or spoken praise, often at a funeral

Euphoric blissful. Synonyms: *buoyant, ebullient, ecstatic, elated, exuberant, exultant, jubilant, rapturous*

Euthanasia the practice of painlessly killing a suffering or terminal (dying) patient. Synonym: *quietus*

Eventuality possibility. Synonym: *contingency*

Everlasting lasting forever. Synonym: *incorruptible.* Antonyms: *ephemeral, evanescent, fleeting, fugitive, impermanent, transient, transitory*

Executive lawmaking or managerial

Existentialism a philosophy that individuals must find their *own* meaning to existence

Exorbitant unfairly high. Synonym: *extortionate*

Exorcise cut out an evil spirit, expel

Exploit use to one's advantage. Synonym: *capitalize on*

Extort steal by force

Extraction removal

Extradition moving of a criminal or criminal suspect from one country to another. Synonyms: *deportation, repatriation*

Extricate get out

Fabricate construct

Fabrication an invented story or excuse, a lie. Synonyms: *equivocation, prevarication*

Fairest beautiful. Synonyms: *pulchritudinous, winsome*

Fascist an oppressive system of government. Synonyms: *authoritarian, despotic, dictatorial, draconian, imperious, totalitarian, tyrannical.* Antonym: *democratic*

Fatuous silly or foolish, pointless. Synonyms: *absurd, asinine, inane, vacuous, vapid*

Fealty loyalty. Synonym: *fidelity*

Federation an allied group of states

Feeble very weak. Synonyms: *frail, impuissant*

Fellowship an association with a shared interest, friendship. Synonyms: *brotherhood, fraternity, guild, sisterhood, sodality, sorority*

Ferocious fierce. Synonyms: *feral, savage, undomesticated*

Fictitious not real

Figuratively not literally (metaphorically). Synonym: *allegorically*

Filch steal

Flabbergasted astonished. Synonyms: *boggled, confounded, dumbfounded, staggered, stupefied*

Foe enemy

Formidable powerful or intimidating. Synonym: *puissant*

Fortitude courage and strength. Synonyms: *audacity, doggedness, doughtiness, grit, indefatigability, intrepidity, mettle, moxie, perseverance, pertinacity, pluck, resolve, steadfastness, tenacity*

Fortuitous lucky

Fulsome excessive, especially regarding flattery. Synonyms: *adulatory, cloying, fawning, ingratiating, obsequious, profuse, saccharine, simpering, smarmy, sycophantic, toady, treacly, unctuous*

Fuselage outer covering of a vehicle or device

Futile pointless. Synonyms: *absurd, fatuous, inane, nugatory, vacuous, vain, vapid*

Gambit a calculated risk taken to gain an advantage in a game, competition, or battle. Synonyms: *machination, maneuver, ploy, ruse, scheme, stratagem, tactic, wangle*

Garrulous talkative. Synonyms: *effusive, expansive, loquacious, prolix, verbose, voluble*. Antonyms: *reticent, taciturn*

Genre category or type

Gilded covered with gold

Glen valley

Goodwill consideration. Synonyms: *amity, benevolence, charity, collaboration*. Antonym: *hostility*

Gothic dark or gloomy; relating to the Goths of Eastern Europe during the Dark Ages. Synonym: *macabre*

Gracious courteous. Synonyms: *amiable, benevolent, chivalrous, civil, cordial, decorous, diplomatic, hospitable, magnanimous, tactful*

Grandiloquent using pompous, fancy language

Greenhorn an inexperienced person. Synonyms: *neophyte, novice, tenderfoot, tyro*

Guffawing laughing loudly

Gustation taste

242

Hackneyed overused

Haggis sheep's intestines and organs mixed with fat, oatmeal, and seasoning, and then boiled in the sheep's stomach.

Hallowed sacred. Synonyms: *consecrated, inviolable, sacrosanct, sanctified*

Harbinger something that signals the approach of something else. Synonyms: *augury, forerunner, foretoken, forewarning, herald, indication, omen, portent, precursor, presage*

Haste a rush

Hayseed a simple, unrefined person from the countryside; a seed obtained from hay

Hedonism philosophy that advocates seeking pleasure

Hermetically completely sealed

Hermit loner. Synonyms: *anchoress, eremite, recluse, troglodyte*

Hokey corny, overused, or overly sentimental

Horde mob. Synonym: *throng*

Hostile unfriendly or even harmful

Hostility unfriendliness or aggression. Synonyms: *acrimony, animosity, antagonism, antipathy, belligerence, enmity, malevolence, malice, rancor, truculence, venom*

Hubris pride. Synonyms: *arrogance, conceit, egotism, haughtiness, hauteur, pomposity, superciliousness*. Antonym: *humility*

Hullabaloo commotion. Synonyms: *brouhaha, clamor, furor, fuss, hoo-hah, hubbub, hurly-burly, mayhem, palaver, pandemonium, ruckus, rumpus, to-do, tumult, turmoil*

Hybrid mixture. Synonyms: *amalgamation, composite, fusion*

Hypnosis an altered, sleep-like state that is very responsive to influence and suggestion

Imminent looming

Immortal never dying. Synonyms: *ceaseless, eternal, everlasting, immutable, imperishable, inextinguishable, intransient, perpetual*. Antonyms: *ephemeral, evanescent, fleeting, mortal, transient*

Impending looming or coming soon. Synonyms: *forthcoming, imminent*

Imperative critically important. Synonym: *vital*

Imperial relating to an empire, bossy, or domineering. Synonym: *imperious*

Imperialist royal or imposing

Impertinence disrespect. Synonyms: *audacity, cheek, effrontery, impudence, insolence, temerity*

Impetuous spontaneous and impulsive. Synonyms: *hasty, heedless, imprudent, precipitate, rash, temerarious, unpremeditated*

Implacable unstoppable or unable to be satisfied. Synonyms: *inexorable, intransigent, relentless, unappeasable*

Implausible unbelievable

Implore beg. Synonyms: *beseech, entreat, importune*

Incision a surgical cut

Incisive sharp-witted and astute

Incisor a sharp tooth in the front of the mouth

Inconsequential not important

Incontrovertible unquestionable. Synonyms: *conclusive, indisputable, indubitable, irrefutable, unassailable*

Incorruptible indestructible. Synonyms: *enduring, everlasting, imperishable, indissoluble*

Incredulous disbelieving

Incursions attacks. Synonyms: *forays, sorties*

Indentured indebted or bound

Indictments accusations of wrongdoing

Indigenous native, home-grown. Synonyms: *aboriginal, autochthonous*

Inevitable unavoidable. Synonyms: *ineludible, inexorable*

Inexorably unavoidably. Synonyms: *implacably, inevitably, interminably, intransigently, irrevocably, relentlessly, unceasingly, unrelentingly, unremittingly*

Infamy fame for something bad

Inglorious shameful, not famous

Inherent natural or inborn. Synonyms: *innate, intrinsic*

Iniquities sins. Synonyms for iniquity: *depravity, impiousness, impropriety, transgression, turpitude, vice, villainy*

Injunction formal order

Innate present from birth or natural. Synonyms: *connate, inborn, inherent, instinctive, intrinsic*

Innocuous harmless. Synonym: *benign*

Innovation change or breakthroughs. Synonym: *ingenuity*

Insidious treacherous and clever. Synonyms: *crafty, cunning, shifty, sly, wily*

Insinuating implying. Synonym: *intimating*

Insipid lacking flavor or spirit. Synonyms: *banal, flat, hackneyed, inane, jejune, pedestrian, tired, trite, vapid*

Insolent rudely disrespectful. Synonyms: *cheeky, contemptuous, contumelious, impertinent, impudent, insubordinate, pert, sassy, saucy*

Insurgents rebels. Synonyms: *agitators, insurrectionists, renegades, subversives*

Intact complete or undamaged

Integrity durability, honesty

Intemperate lacking self-control. Synonyms: *immoderate, prodigal, profligate, unrestrained, wanton*

Interminable endless. Synonyms: *ceaseless, eternal, incessant*. Antonym: *ephemeral*

Invincible undefeatable. Synonyms: *impregnable, incontrovertible, indomitable, inviolable, unassailable*

Irrelevant unimportant. Synonyms: *immaterial, inapposite*

Irreverence disrespect and lack of seriousness. Synonyms: *contempt, flippancy, impertinence, impudence, insolence*

Irrevocable permanent, not reversible. Synonyms: *binding, immutable, incontrovertible, peremptory, unalterable*. Antonym: *temporary*

Jerkwater a small, unimportant, and out-of-the-way town

Judicious sensible. Synonyms: *astute, canny, discerning, percipient, politic, prudent, sagacious, shrewd*

Kaput useless

Lackeys followers

Lament grieve

Lateral on the side or sideways

Legacy something passed down. Synonym: *heritage*

Lethal deadly

Levity humor. Synonyms: *frivolity, gaiety, glee, jocularity, jollity, joviality, lightheartedness, merriment, mirth*. Antonyms: *gravitas, gravity*

Liaison representative or ambassador, a secret love affair

Loquacious talkative. Synonyms: *effusive, expansive, garrulous, prolix, verbose, voluble*. Antonyms: *reticent, taciturn*

Luminary a person who enlightens and inspires others

Luminous radiant

Macabre deathly and horrifying. Synonyms: *ghastly, gory, grisly, grotesque, gruesome, hideous, morbid*

Maiden first, unmarried, pertaining to a young woman. Synonyms: *inaugural, virgin*

Majestic beautiful, dignified, or regal. Synonyms: *august, distinguished, noble, resplendent, stately, sumptuous*

Malaise unhappiness. Synonym: *melancholy*

Malice ill will. Synonyms: *animus, enmity, maleficence, malevolence, malignity, rancor, spite, vengefulness, vindictiveness.* Antonym: *benevolence (good will)*

Malignant harmful. Antonym: *benign*

Malleable flexible or easily bent. Synonyms: *compliant, ductile, pliable, tractable.* Antonym: *intractable*

Mandate formal order. Synonyms: *decree, directive, edict, fiat, injunction, proclamation*

Marginally slightly

Martinet strict disciplinarian. Synonyms: *doctrinaire, dogmatist, pedant, stickler*

Material physical things, such as possessions. Synonyms: *corporeal, earthly, mundane, physical, secular, tangible, temporal, worldly.* Antonym: *spiritual*

Matriarchy rule by women

Mawkishness emotional sappiness. Synonyms for mawkish: *cloying, overly sentimental, saccharine, treacly*

Maxim concise, meaningful statement of truth. Synonyms: *adage, aphorism, apothegm, axiom, dictum, epigram, precept, proverb, saw, truism*

Mayhem disorder. Synonyms: *anarchy, bedlam, chaos, pandemonium, turmoil*

Ménage members of a household

Ménage à trois three people together in a sexual relationship

Menagerie collection of diverse people, animals, or things

Mentor teacher or guide

Mercenaries hired soldiers. Synonym: *condottiere*

Merciless pitiless. Synonyms: *callous, heartless, ruthless*

Metaphorically not literally

Metamorphosis change of shape or form

Micturated urinated. Synonym: *emictated*

Mired slowed down

Mogul powerful person

Monarchy rule by one—usually by a king or queen

Moniker nickname. Synonyms: *pseudonym, sobriquet*

Morpheus the Greek god of dreams

Morphology the study of word forms and word relationships

Myopic focused on the short term, nearsighted

Nacelles streamlined casings (material that encloses) of an engine

Narcolepsy the disorder of falling asleep uncontrollably whenever relaxed

Nefarious wicked. Synonyms: *baleful, depraved, heinous, impious, iniquitous, malevolent, pernicious*

Neglectful not caring for properly. Synonyms: *disregarding, negligent*

Nocuous harmful

Normative relating to what is the norm. Synonyms for norm: *convention, exemplar*

Notoriously well known for bad things. Synonyms: *infamously, scandalously*

Nugatory meaningless

Obsequious overly submissive

Officious annoyingly interfering and domineering. Synonyms: *bumptious, meddlesome, overbearing, overzealous*

Oleaginous overly submissive

Olfaction sense of smell

Oligarchy rule by a small group of individuals

Oppression cruel and unfair use of power. Synonyms: *despotism, persecution, repression, subjection, subjugation, suppression, tyranny.* Antonym: *freedom*

Oral relating to the mouth

Orbit track

Ostentatious showy. Synonyms: *brash, flamboyant, gaudy, ornate, pretentious, vulgar*

Parable moral story

Paradox contradiction

Pardoned freed of blame. Synonyms: *absolved, acquitted, exculpated, exonerated, vindicated.* Antonym: *condemned*

Pariah outcast. Synonym: *persona non grata*

Parity equality

Parlance slang. Synonym: *jargon*

Parody imitate in a funny way

Pedantic annoyingly precise. Synonyms: *captious, fastidious, finicky, fussy, meticulous, perfectionist, persnickety, punctilious, scrupulous*

Penchant fondness for or tendency. Synonyms: *knack, predilection, proclivity*

Pensive introspective or thoughtful. Synonyms: *brooding, contemplative, meditative, musing, reflective, ruminative*

Penurious penniless or cheap

Perpetuates continues

Persona non grata an unwelcome person. Synonyms: *outcast, pariah*

Pertinent relevant. Synonyms: *apposite, apropos, germane*

Perversions misuse or corruption of things

Pheromone chemicals that animals secrete to effect other animals of their species

Phonology the study of speech sounds of a language

Pilfer steal

Pinnacle highest point. Synonyms: *acme, apex, apogee, capstone, crest, peak, summit, zenith.* Antonym: *nadir*

Pioneer originator, first developer. Synonym: *progenitor*

Pissant worthless. Synonym: *nugatory*

Pithy short and meaningful, Synonyms: *compendious, concise, crisp, epigrammatic, succinct, terse.* Antonym: *verbose*

Placate satisfy or soothe

Platitudinous overused

Plutarchy rule by the wealthy

Podunk a small, unimportant, and boring town

Polity government

Polyglot a person who speaks many languages

Polyvalent having many forms or values

Ponder think deeply

Ponderous heavy and awkward or dull. Synonyms: *laborious, lifeless, maladroit, monotonous, pedestrian, plodding, stilted, stodgy, tedious.* Antonym: *animated*

Pontificating annoyingly preachy. Synonym: *dogmatizing*

Postulated suggested. Synonyms: *hypothesized, posited, proposed*

Potent powerful. Synonyms: *formidable, puissant*

Precedent an earlier example

Precocious mature at an early age

Prelude introduction

Pretentious snobby, showy, or conceited, especially in an attempt to impress. Synonyms: *affected, ostentatious, pompous*

Probation period of testing or observation

Prodigal wasteful or overly extravagant. Synonym: *profligate*

Progenitor originator. Synonym: *pioneer*

Prospered thrived. Synonyms: *blossomed, burgeoned, flourished*

Protocol rules for behavior, procedures. Synonyms: *conventions, decorum, etiquette, proprieties, punctilio*

Provincial narrow-minded or unsophisticated. Synonyms: *insular, parochial*

Prudent sensible, especially with regard to future outcomes. Synonyms: *astute, judicious, sagacious, shrewd.* Antonym: *myopic (focused on the short term, rather than the future; nearsighted)*

Prurient excessively sexual, immoral. Synonyms: *concupiscent, lascivious, lewd, libidinous, licentious, lubricious, salacious*

Psalms sacred songs or hymns

Pseudo fake. Synonyms: *bogus, contrived, ersatz, mock, phony, sham, spurious*

Psychosomatic physical illnesses that are actually caused by the mind

Pugnacious eager to fight

Pungent strong or sharp. Synonyms: *acerbic, acrimonious, biting, caustic, incisive, sarcastic, sardonic, scathing, trenchant, venomous*

Qualifiedly with reservation

Quasi supposed or partial

Queried questioned

Query question

Ramifications consequences, usually negative

Ravenous famished. Synonyms: *gluttonous, greedy, insatiable, voracious*

Recluse hermit

Reconcile settle, reunite

Redemption forgiveness for or salvation from sin. Synonym: *absolution*

Regurgitation vomiting

Reign rule

Relativistic not set, but related to other factors

Relentlessly constantly or tirelessly. Synonyms: *incessantly, inexorably, interminably, unremitting*

Render create

Rendezvous meet up

Rendition secretly moving a criminal or criminal suspect from one country to another

Repartee wordplay, banter

Replete full

Repressed put down or subdued. Synonyms: *oppressed, subdued, subjugated, tyrannized*

Reprisals acts of revenge or payback. Synonyms: *requital, retaliation, retribution, vengeance*

Reproach blame or scolding. Synonyms: *admonishment, censure, rebuke, reprimand, reproof*

Republic a government ruled by its people or by an elected ruler

Resourcefulness the ability to creatively solve problems. Synonyms: *enterprise, gumption, ingenuity, initiative, inventiveness*

Revelation surprising or dramatic announcement or realization. Synonym: *epiphany*

Revoke cancel. Synonym: *countermand*

Righteous moral or honorable. Synonyms: *ethical, scrupulous, upright, virtuous*

Saccharine overly sweet or sentimental. Synonyms: *cloying, mawkish, treacly*

Sack steal

Satchel a bag that is carried by a long strap over the shoulder. Synonyms: *man purse, murse (just kidding)*

Savvy intelligent and insightful. Synonyms: *canny, incisive, judicious, keen, perspicacious, sagacious, sage, shrewd, wise.* Antonym: *obtuse*

Schisms divided groups based on differences of opinion. Synonyms for schism: *breach, break, chasm, disagreement, discord, dissension, gulf, rift, rupture, separation, severance*

Scourge something that causes great difficulty. Synonyms: *affliction, bane, blight, menace, plague*

Scribe a secretary or any person who writes

Sedition inciting rebellion. Synonyms: *insurgence, insurrection, mutiny, perfidy, subversion, treason*

Seraphim angel. Synonym: *cherubim*

Serendipitous lucky. Synonyms: *auspicious, felicitous, fortuitous, opportune, propitious*

Servile overly submissive

Simpering insincerely and flirtatiously cute and shy

Socialism an economic system in which all people own all property together

Solemn serious. Synonyms: *earnest, grave, sober, somber*

Sonar the system of using sound to locate objects in one's environment

Sonic relating to sound

Soporific sleep inducing. Synonyms: *somniferous, somnolent*

Sovereign ruler. Synonyms: *monarch, potentate*

Subtleties clever methods of achieving something; small or understated distinctions between things. Synonyms for subtlety: *canniness, percipience, perspicacity, shrewdness*

Sully dirty. Synonyms: *befoul, besmirch, blemish, defile, mar, pollute, stain, soil, spoil, taint, tarnish*

Supplant replace, usually by force. Synonyms: *displace, supersede, usurp*

Supple soft, flexible, and graceful. Synonyms: *agile, limber, lissome, lithe, malleable, nimble, pliable, pliant, willowy*. Antonym: *rigid*

Supreme highest

Sycophantic flattering to get something from someone of power

Symbiont mutually beneficial

Symbiotic mutually beneficial relationship

Symmetrical evenly proportioned

Sympathy compassion

Synergy cooperation

Syndicate an association of people promoting similar interests

Syntax arranging words together to make well-formed sentences

Synthesis the uniting of parts into a whole

Systematic organized. Synonym: *methodical*

Tactile touchable, relating to the sense or touch. Synonyms: *corporeal, palpable, tangible*

Tedious boring. Synonyms: *insipid, lackluster, monochrome, monotonous, mundane, pedestrian, vapid*. Antonym: *exciting*

Temper counterbalance or soften

Temperance self-restraint

Temperate mild, restrained, or mild-mannered. Synonym: *clement*

Terrorism using intimidation, and usually violence, to achieve political goals

Thwart prevent or block progress of. Synonyms: *forestall, stonewall, stymie*

Titan person of tremendous power or significance

Toady overly submissive

Transcribe copy or put thoughts, notes, or speech into writing

Transcriptions written symbols or words

Transient wandering, temporary. Synonym: *itinerant*

Transitory temporary

Translucent allowing light but not images through

Treason disloyalty to one's country. Synonyms: *perfidy, sedition*

Trepidation fear. Synonyms: *apprehension, disquiet, foreboding*

Trite overused

Tropical from the tropics (near the equator); literally, the area on the planet between the Tropic of Cancer and the Tropic of Capricorn

Truculent eager to fight

Tyrannical oppressive and controlling. Synonyms: *authoritarian, despotic, dictatorial, draconian, fascist, illiberal, imperious, totalitarian.*

Tyranny cruel and harsh leadership. Synonyms: *authoritarianism, despotism, Fascism, oppression, subjugation, totalitarianism*

Umbrage anger and annoyance

Unequivocally definitely. Synonyms: *categorically, incontrovertibly, indubitably, unconditionally, unqualifiedly*

Unethical not moral

Unkempt untidy

Unparalleled having no parallel or equal. Synonyms: *elite, exceptional, nonpareil, singular, unprecedented*

Unprecedented totally new, never seen before

Unqualified absolute; untrained or unable. Synonyms: *categorical, unconditional, unequivocal, unmitigated, untempered*

Ushers in begins, guides in. Synonym: *heralds*

Uvula the fleshy thing that dangles in the back of your throat

Vacuous mindless or empty. Synonyms: *fatuous, inane, insipid, vacant, vapid.* Antonym: *intelligent*

Vacuum totally empty space

Vagaries unexpected changes. Synonyms: *caprice, eccentricities, fluctuations, foibles, peculiarities, quirks, whimsy*

Vagrant a homeless person who wanders

Valor bravery. Synonyms: *audacity, courage, dauntlessness, gallantry, moxie, pluck.* Antonym: *cowardice*

Valorous brave

Vanguarding promoting

Vanity pride or egotism

Vanquish defeat

Vaudevillian relating to entertainment variety shows from the 1920s that were called "vaudeville"

Venal corrupt

Veneer fake surface

Vengeance revenge. Synonyms: *reprisal, requital, retaliation, retribution*

Verbiage wordiness

Verbose wordy. Synonyms: *effusive, expansive, garrulous, loquacious, prolix, voluble.* Antonyms: *concise, laconic, reticent, succinct, taciturn*

Vergence coming together; medical term for when the pupils of the eyes move together in unison either toward or away from each other

Verify confirm the truth of

Verisimilitude the appearance of being real or true. Synonyms: *credibility, plausibility*

Verity a fundamental truth

Vesper evening prayer

Vessel container

Vestige remainder

Vetted carefully examined. Synonym: *scrutinized*

Vexation frustration, annoyance, or worry

Viable possible. Synonym: *feasible*

Vicariously instead of another; experiencing something through someone else

Vice wickedness

Vicissitudes changes, usually for the worse

Victor winner or conqueror. Synonym: *vanquisher*

Vile very unpleasant, evil

Virile manly, strong, and energetic; with a strong sex drive

Virtues good qualities. Antonym: *vices (bad qualities)*

Virulent hostile

Visage face

Viscosity gooeyness

Vital essential. Synonym: *imperative*

Vivid bright, clear, or lively

Vivified enlivened

Vocations occupations that people are well suited for or even "called" to do. Synonym: *métiers*

Void a completely empty space.
Synonym: *vacuum*

Volition will

Voracious greedy

Vouchsafing revealing or granting

Vox populi Latin word meaning "voice of the people" (it refers to popular opinion)

Wanton deliberately spiteful or promiscuous

Wariness cautiousness

Whim sudden urge. Synonyms: *caprice, fickleness, foible, megrim, vagary*

Whimsical acting on urges.
Synonyms: *capricious, erratic, fickle, inconstant, mercurial, mutable, protean, volatile*

Whistle-stop a small, unimportant town; the brief stops of a campaigning politician

Wily clever and devious.
Synonyms: *artful, calculating, crafty, cunning, foxy, machinating, scheming, sly*

Xenolinguistics the study of alien languages

Xenophobic afraid of foreigners